Praise for *It's a God Thing, Volume 2*

"Don Jacobson has done a mighty thing. He has compiled stories of faith for all of us who believe God still answers those who call on Him and proves trustworthy to those who trust in Him. Whether you see these stories as miracles or examples of God's faithfulness, you are sure to be challenged and inspired. *It's a God Thing, Volume 2* reminds us God still moves mountains."

> — Ken Wytsma, lead pastor, Antioch Church, Bend, OR; president, Kilns College; and author, *The Grand Paradox: The Messiness of Life, the Mystery of God and the Necessity of Faith*

"Many question if miracles really are for today. As you read account after account of these miracle stories, there is a common thread of the goodness and grace of God. Let these accounts inspire your faith to reach out and make a miracle part of your story."

> — Julia Immonen, double world record Atlantic rower; Sport for Freedom founder; and author, *Row for Freedom: Crossing an Ocean in Search of Hope*

"I hear it all the time: 'I can't watch the news because it is too depressing,' or 'All they report is bad news.' But there is good news, and my friend Don Jacobson and the folks at K-LOVE want you to know that God is still in control. *It's a God Thing, Volume 2* is an inspiring collection of love, hope, and grace stories lived out through His children. Be encouraged. God is there even when He is most difficult to see. These amazing stories will remind you of that truth."

"It isn't often I find myself holding my breath while reading a book, yet that's exactly what I found myself doing again and again as I turned the pages of this book. It's one thing *to hear* a moving story; it's quite another *to be moved by* a story in a way that simultaneously challenges and stimulates your faith. My friend Don Jacobson accomplishes exactly that with his latest compilation."

— Sami Cone, blogger (SamiCone. com); TV personality; and radio host, nationally syndicated *Family Money Minute*

"We all have a God Thing story in our own lives. Sometimes seeing God's work in others allows us to look introspectively on the miracles He's done in us."

— Mark Batterson, lead pastor, National Community Church, Washington DC; and author, *The Circle Maker: Praying Circles Around Your Biggest Dreams and Greatest Fears*

"The writer of Hebrews exhorts Christians to encourage one another (Heb. 10:24–25). *It's a God Thing, Volume 2* encourages Christians with stories from the lives of everyday believers that remind us that we serve a God who loves to show up. If you're discouraged, this is the book for you. If someone you know or love is discouraged, this is the book they need."

— Ed Underwood, senior pastor, Church of the Open Door, Glendora, CA; and author, *When God Breaks Your Heart* and *The Trail: A Tale about Discovering God's Will*

"If testimony is evidence or proof of the existence of something, then recounting the greatness of God in our own stories demonstrates His faithfulness again and again. In *It's a God Thing, Volume 2* Don Jacobson and K-LOVE have assembled an electrifying collection of personal testimonies that is uplifting and ignites greater faith with each successive story. Whether you're looking to combat doubt or fortify your faith, *It's a God Thing* boldly declares the goodness of a God who goes beyond our understanding and dances with the miraculous."

> — Logan Wolfram, blogger
> (loganwolfram.com); writer;
> and executive director, Allume
> Conference

"With their new book, *It's a God Thing,* I believe K-LOVE and my friend Don Jacobson will call friends of Jesus everywhere to look for His capers around the world! Do you know why God involves Himself in our lives? Because God is love and love does!"

> — Bob Goff, author of the *New York Times* bestseller *Love Does*

"If there is one thing that God wants us to understand, it is total dependence on Him. Sometimes we find that we are completely wiped out and feel there is nowhere else to turn. God tells us to turn it all over to Him; it is then that He says He will take care of us. In Him is where we find true peace that passes understanding, when we trade our own understanding for our Father's. The stories in this book demonstrate that. These true servants of God share how their lives were transformed when their understanding became the Father's. What a blessing to be a child of the King!"

> — Missy Robertson, star of *Duck Dynasty*

"There is so much going on around us that we never see. Life is all about perspective, and when that lines up with the hand of God, it is remarkable to witness. This book and collection of stories from my friends at K-LOVE will inspire and encourage you greatly!"

> — Andy Andrews, *New York Times* best-selling author, *The Noticer* and *The Traveler's Gift*

"Every day we all are faced with stress, situations we can't control and often the fear that we really are all alone. God clearly calls us to be *one body*. He wants us to come together—to tell our stories—to encourage and support each other. That is what these stories do—they give us courage in times of peril and strengthen us when we feel helpless. God has not left us alone—He is with us."

— TobyMac, top Christian artist and
Grammy Award winner

"When my work started taking me to remote communities across Africa, Latin America, and Asia, I began hearing more and more about real miracles—God's intervention into the everyday on behalf of his people. For various reasons we in the West have forgotten how to see this evidence of God's hand on our lives—whether in big or small ways. In Don Jacobson's *It's a God Thing*, we are given the gift of a stirring collage of everyday miracles that encourage and inspire while also sensitizing us to the reality that God is still at work in incredible ways in our lives and around the world."

— Keith Wright, president, Food for
the Hungry

"*It's a God Thing* is a refreshing reminder of God's attention to the details of our lives. In a world that is often filled with an excess of bad news, the accounts of everyday miracles point to the bigness of God and the greatness of His mercy. My only complaint is that the book ended too soon!"

— Vicki Courtney, speaker and
best-selling author, *Your Girl*,
TeenVirtue, and *5 Conversations
You Must Have With Your Daughter*

"Most of us, including myself, see miracles as something only happening during biblical times. Well, my friend, since the Bible applies today more than ever, I'd say we are still in biblical times, and miracles are very much alive and well! We've just gotten really good at explaining away miracles, no matter how big or small. My prayer is this book opens our eyes to the miracles that happen around us and even in our own lives. For me, the timing of this book is absolutely perfect. Sometimes I'm guilty of looking so hard for God that I miss Him right in front of me. May we all be reminded through *It's a God Thing* that some of the simplest moments in life can quite possibly be some of God's greatest miracles. Because of the cross, my very next breath is a *huge* miracle. Thank you, Jesus!"

— Bart Millard, lead singer of MercyMe

"There is nothing better than hearing others talk about the ways that God has intervened in their lives. Miracles happen every day all around the world. These stories are incredible."

— Robert D. Smith, author, *20,000 Days and Counting*

"Through everyday miracles discovered in the nooks and crannies of life, *It's a God Thing* presents a stunning glimpse of God through the lives of people like you and me. *It's a God Thing* is more than a book. It's an invitation, an encounter, a way of life. I recommend it highly."

— Stephan Bauman, president and CEO, World Relief

"Nothing astonished people in the New Testament more than watching Jesus perform a miracle right before their eyes—and nothing inspires us today more than hearing He did it again! My good friend Don Jacobson, publisher of *The Prayer of Jabez*, has once again launched the perfect message for today—don't miss it!"

— Bruce Wilkinson, author, *The Prayer of Jabez*

"This book is an unbelievable reminder of God's power and presence. These testimonies show how alive and active God is in our daily lives. Story upon story affirms to me that from the beginning to the end, God is with us and for us. Whether we are running out of a burning building, drowning, or need just a small whisper of encouragement, we can be confident that He will never leave us or forsake us. The ministry of K-LOVE and its listeners inspire me to be bold and courageous in sharing the love of Jesus."

— Michael McDowell, NASCAR
Sprint Cup Series driver

"God doesn't need for us to be aware of the miracles He's performing, but they're happening every day! *It's a God Thing*, a new book from K-LOVE, is a powerful vehicle to tell the story of a number of those miracles."

— Brandon Heath, 2008 New Artist
of the Year Dove Award winner

VOLUME 2

VOLUME 2

WHEN MIRACLES HAPPEN
TO EVERYDAY PEOPLE

CREATED BY

DON JACOBSON AND K-LOVE

W Publishing Group

An Imprint of Thomas Nelson

Published in Nashville, Tennessee, by W Publishing, an imprint of Thomas Nelson.

Thomas Nelson titles may be purchased in bulk for educational, business, fund-raising, or sales promotional use. For information, please e-mail SpecialMarkets@ ThomasNelson.com.

Library of Congress Control Number: 2014912710

ISBN 978-0-529-10551-6

Printed in the United States of America

14 15 16 17 RRD 5 4 3 2 1

It's a God Thing, Volume 2 is dedicated to the faithful listeners and supporters of K-LOVE.

Many of these stories are yours, and the telling of them will refresh and encourage people everywhere.

Thank you.

Contents

Contents

Acknowledgments

The family of God is an amazing group of people who every day sacrifice, share, and make meaningful connections in the pursuit of making Jesus known. The collective stories in a book like *It's a God Thing, Volume 2* simply would not be possible without acknowledging the amazing God whom we serve and His people's willingness to share what He is doing in their lives.

So we would like to thank . . .

our great God and Savior, Jesus Christ—these
    stories begin and end with You
each of the contributing authors whose stories
    appear in this second volume
Craig Borlase, the writer who helped craft their
    stories

Christine Metcalf for her skillful editing
the W Publishing Group at Thomas Nelson—
  partnering with you is a joy

We are deeply grateful for each of you.

Introduction

Stories that show how God is at work around the world can't help but bring encouragement to readers. And that's exactly what we have seen with the first volume of *It's a God Thing*. Reader reviews have brought tears of joy to our eyes and prayers of thankfulness that we have been a part of bringing light to people who have experienced, will experience, or are experiencing a dark time in their lives.

Following are a few quotes from reviewers of the first volume:

- Loved this book! I laughed and cried, sometimes all at once!
- This book was amazing and so inspiring! It was hard to put down—it gave me hope and deepened my faith!
- This is a very inspiring book of true-life God stories. A wonderful read about how God showed up in such a real way. Highly recommend!

- Full of hope and amazing miracles! Thank you for putting this book together! I can't wait to read the next book!
- I love reading the positive and encouraging stories in this book and how God always has our best interests in mind.
- I love this book!! It's so encouraging and inspiring to read about miracles that are happening today!
- Thank you for the compilation—such a great reminder that God is constantly involved in the small details of our everyday lives. An encouraging and compelling read . . . thanks.

As you read these next stories in this second volume, our prayer for you is that you will be awakened to see God at work in your life as well.

Blessings on your way.

1

Rescued

Susie Whitten

The old truck was struggling up the dirt road that wound up the hill, but it was a beautiful summer day to be out with the family. It was 1976, and my husband, Steve, was driving the liquid feed truck for my dad, delivering feed to dairy farms for their cattle. With our two-year-old daughter, Robyn, standing between us in the cab and the tank full of liquid, we were slowly making the delivery to a ranch high in the Chino Hills of Southern California. It was so warm that day, and the higher we climbed in the old International truck, the hotter it seemed to get.

Near the top of the hill, just as the pull of the tank was at its peak, we heard a *pop* from beneath the truck. Instantly Steve stepped on the brakes. Nothing happened. The truck slowed under the weight of the load, and Steve threw me an anxious glance. "Jump out," he said, "and get some rocks for behind the tires."

As soon as I opened the door and started to get out, the

truck began rolling backward. Steve was standing on the brakes with all his might, and with the open door pushing at my back, forcing me along with it, I knew I had to reach in and grab Robyn. Everything was happening so fast, and our little girl panicked and grabbed hold of Steve. "Go to Mommy," he called, pushing her back toward me.

By now the truck was moving so fast that I had to run to keep up, my feet slipping on the dirt track. Screaming at Steve to get out, I pulled Robyn by the legs as hard as I could. As soon as she was free, the truck seemed to surge back with even greater power. The open door knocked Robyn and me to the ground. I looked up and watched as Steve, still standing on the brakes, his face straining with all he had, continued backward. As the road twisted off to the side, the truck carried on, disappearing from view.

I screamed as I ran to the edge. I looked down and watched as the truck rolled over and over, tearing up the shrubbery, flipping from end to end with great clouds of dust swirling up into the air before settling four hundred feet below. I stood there with Robyn, holding her close. We were in shock, covered in blood, dirt, and dust from our fall. It was all too much to take in.

Suddenly Steve was next to us. There was not a speck of dust on his white T-shirt and white cord jeans. "How did you get here?" I asked.

"I don't know," he said, looking even more shocked than I felt. "I think God took me out of the truck." We looked down to see our house and car keys on the ground by our feet. We hugged and wept for a while and then started our long walk back down the dirt road to try and find help.

A man working in a nearby barn took us to my sister's house, from where we went to the doctor to get Robyn's and my wounds cleaned up. We told him our story, and as he looked at Steve, he warned him that tomorrow he'd feel pretty sore. We could tell he wasn't quite sure what to make of our story, and he told Steve that it would have been the adrenaline rush that got him out of the truck so quickly. Once it wore off, he could expect to feel sore.

We knew better. I had seen Steve in the truck as it went backward over the edge. I knew that the windows were up, and by that time, if he had managed to open a door, it would have knocked him down to the ground in an instant. There was just no way he could have made his own escape from the truck without so much as a speck of dirt on his clothes.

The next day Steve didn't have a sore muscle in his body. As he and my dad hiked down to the truck to make plans to get it out, they saw the broken driveshaft and mangled brake clamp. And they saw that even though his window was broken out, it was still in a rolled-up position with the door shut.

We knew right then, as we still know today, that God took him out of that truck. God chose to spare Steve's life because He wasn't done with my husband here on earth yet. How He did it, we don't know. But we do know that it was God and God alone.

Prisoners of Hope

Tami Byrd

It took only two days of a painful ankle for our entire world to be thrown into chaos. Before our oldest son started to complain that he was feeling sore, we had been just another growing family. Blase was four, his little brother was three, and I was five months pregnant with our third child. Life was full, chaotic, and wonderful.

Then on December 3, 2006, as Blase sat nursing his foot, I listened to a doctor deliver his diagnosis: an extremely rare form of leukemia. He had been healthy and active since birth, and the doctor's words stunned us. That numbness soon gave way to a series of overwhelming emotions as my husband and I felt our lives overrun by fear and terror.

The six months following the diagnosis were the hardest I have ever lived through. Blase was given extremely intense chemotherapy, but even with all the drugs being pumped into him, the doctors could only tell us that he had a 20 to 30 percent chance of surviving five more years "*if* he makes it through the treatment," they said. The chemo had been made for—and tested on—adults, not kids.

We were told that three and a half more years of chemo-therapy, mostly inpatient, lay ahead of us. The side effects were frightening and gruesome, including brain damage, caused by the chemo being administered directly into the fluid surrounding the brain and spinal cord; paralysis; organ failure; sepsis; learning disabilities; drop foot; and a hundred other things. The fear grew even greater, and we prayed like crazy though we had no idea where God was in everything. He seemed distant, almost as though He had abandoned us. What we knew for sure was that we felt helpless.

Still we carried on, praying. Hundreds of people joined us, and we had Blase blessed by pastors and priests. Not a single day or night passed that I was not on my knees, crying out to God. And when we got tired or too discouraged to stand, many of our friends carried us along with their love and support.

As my first son fought for his life and my third child grew within me, the doctors told me that there was the possibility that my yet-to-be-born baby might be able to help. If the baby I was carrying was a bone marrow match to our ill son, they could use the umbilical cord to do a bone marrow transplant in hopes of a cure. Again they stressed that word *if.* I asked what would happen if it wasn't a match. Was there a chance of some other donor's bone marrow being used? "No," they said. "We won't consider a bone marrow transplant from anyone other than Blase's parents or siblings. The risk of death is too high."

"Okay," I said. "If this baby is a match, what's the chance of success?"

"If your son does end up having the transplant, the mortality rate is near 50 percent."

The bone marrow transplant team at the University of Michigan told us that while they carried out two hundred fifty transplants a year and had seen lots of pregnant moms, they had never seen a mom carrying a child that was a match to her ill child. They put the chances of a match at less than 25 percent. Searching for something to hold on to, we asked what the best-case scenario was.

"We never use the word *cured* in relation to a diagnosis like this. He may go into remission, but he will never be cured."

It felt as though our lives were full of big *ifs* and bad odds.

We couldn't understand why God would take one of our children and give us another. As much as we tried to be patient and trust God, we did not understand. We were broken; that was all there was to say.

In March 2007, I gave birth to our third beautiful baby boy. He was absolutely angelic from birth, but we had to wait until May to find out that his umbilical cord blood wasn't just a good match for our oldest son—it was perfect. The doctors had never seen this happen before and proceeded with the transplant in June 2007, making Blase, what we believe to be, the first recipient of sibling cord blood ever performed at U of M. And within just six months, his recovery was so advanced that he was taken off every single medicine and able to start kindergarten.

That was seven years ago, and these days our three boys are just as precious and healthy as they've ever been. And they have a baby sister too! And just last summer, during our son's annual checkup, we sat in the office of the same wonderful doctor who had told us never to expect a cure.

"Well," he said, a smile forming on his face, "he's cured! You don't ever need to come back to the Cancer Center for a checkup again."

Despite the well-documented effects of chemo and radiation on a young child's developing organs, Blase has absolutely no side effects from the treatment he endured.

I can't say the same about our faith though. The whole period has shaped and molded us, leaving deep and lasting marks on how we see our God. For a period of time we felt so alone and forsaken, and it wasn't until many months later that we realized God's hand was on us the whole time. We don't believe God necessarily causes bad things to happen, but He certainly can make a way to almost forget they were ever there.

Our third pregnancy was entirely unplanned. I love the fact that God sent us the answer and set in place the rescue long before we even knew we had a problem. Trust God, no matter what the circumstances. He knows what you need.

Riches in the Rubble

Kellie White

Two hours after the tornado hit, I left my office in Moore and headed south. Crossing the path that the twister had taken as it sliced through the southwest corner of the city, my ten-mile journey home gave me a firsthand view of the absolute devastation and chaos that had been left behind. I saw homes that hadn't just been flattened—they had been destroyed. The storm had eaten up everything in its path.

I stopped for a while in a neighborhood that was home to two foster families with whom I work. As the evening tracked by, I helped them as much as I could. Downed telephone lines, smashed vehicles, dazed people, and tons of debris were spread all over the ground; it took hours to get around and help reunite families with their children. Over the course of the evening, I felt sustained by the knowledge that—thanks to God's grace—I was in the right place at the right time.

I'm a fixer, and I pride myself on being an efficient, capable person. I love to help people in any way I possibly can, so the next day after work, I loaded up my backpack with hamburgers and water and returned to the neighborhood. Although I had gotten a glimpse of the devastation the evening before, I really didn't know what to expect when I encountered people I didn't know. How would I be able to help them?

By the time I arrived, the perimeter of the neighborhood had been barricaded to stop all nonessential vehicles from entering the area. There were so many electrical wires down, so much debris, and cars mangled beyond recognition that it just wasn't safe to have lots of people driving around. So I parked my car and walked through.

The previous day I had been shocked by the state of the houses, but this time it was the state of the people that I found so disturbing. So many faces told the story of the trauma they were enduring, and so many people looked helpless. One man, standing in front of his home, fingers clasped on his head, just stared, tears in his eyes. I offered him food and water. He couldn't speak. He just shook his head and smiled.

Most were like that first man and graciously declined any help. Instead, they continued to try and sift through the piles of rubble they once called home. By the time I reached the end of the street, I could feel the tears welling up in my eyes. I, too, felt helpless. In that moment I realized that on my own, I could do absolutely nothing. But with God I could do anything. For too long I had been relying on my own strengths and abilities to get me through. I had gotten out of the habit of asking God for help. I had started to believe that I could do it on my own.

Standing at the end of the street, a backpack full of

unwanted burgers and bottles of water, staring at a scene of devastation that I could do nothing to put right, I cried. I was inadequate, unable to help. So I prayed.

"Lord, I can't do this. It's overwhelming! Please help me go to the people that You want me to serve and help. Guide me, please. I'm desperate!"

I shouldered my backpack and began walking slowly down the street. When I came to the next corner, I threw up a quick prayer. "Lord, should I go down this road?" I didn't really expect a specific answer, but I got one all the same.

No. Not this one. It was almost like the audible voice of a person right next to me. I was thrilled and sensed God's presence with me more than I ever had in my life. I moved on to the next street and repeated my question.

"This one?"

And again, the same response: *No. Not this one.* A third time and the same thing happened. It was at the fourth street that I finally heard, *Yes. This one.*

The scene was the same that I had witnessed all along. Piles of timber, earth, and household possessions all blended together on the lots. I talked briefly with a family who then immediately got back to work. Then I walked up to a woman dressed in pink with her hair pulled back and thick work gloves on. She was covered in mud and had obviously been working for hours. I greeted her with my usual, "Ma'am, are you hungry or thirsty? I've got some burgers and water."

"I just ate something," she said. "But thanks so much for asking." She kept eye contact with me, and I sensed this was where God had led me. I asked if she could use an extra set of hands, and she quickly said yes. Was she looking for something specific in this pile of splinters, shards of glass, mud, and a beat-up truck where the living room once was?

"I'm looking for special things," she said. So I pulled on the gloves I had thrown into my backpack at the last second and began looking. I had the impression that she was looking for something in particular, but for some reason wasn't yet willing to tell me what that was. And understandably so; I was a stranger, and this was her home we were sifting through.

An hour and a half went by and almost nothing came up. There was a baby photo of her son, a cake server with a pearl handle, all kinds of special things, but none of them got the reaction that told me we were done. I stopped for a drink of water and threw up another desperate plea to God. *Lord, I'm not making a difference! Surely there's more. This woman is obviously looking for something specific, but I don't know what it is. You know what it is, and You know where it is. Could You please help me find it?*

I finished my bottle of water, looked around, and noticed a pile of debris that was still untouched. I walked over, moved the splintered door that was lying on top of the pile, then a few clothes that were lying there in the dirt. And then I saw it. I knew instantly that this was what the woman had been looking for: a once-white envelope, now covered in mud, about three-quarters-of-an-inch thick. The flap was folded under, and I could see it contained a lot of cash. I picked it up and instantly saw another behind it. And then another. All in all, there were seven of them, and they must have contained thousands of dollars. Holding them in my hands, my mouth wide-open, I called out to the woman.

"Ma'am, I found . . . something . . . special."

She caught my gaze, and immediately she knew what I had found. She ran over, and as I opened my hands to show her, she began crying. Between the sobs, she simply said, "That is what I've been searching for. It's my life savings. Thank you so much!" I told her that God had found it for her and that I simply had the privilege of being His hands at that moment.

I've been a Christian for more than thirty years, and I have tried to walk closely with the Lord all that time. But these last three years have been very difficult for our family. I have allowed my relationship with God to relax, to grow a little stale. Where once I heard His voice loud and clear—or still and small—my own voice had become the dominant one in my life.

That day, spent digging in the debris, I realized something with my heart that I've known with my head for thirty years. Before we can be filled with God, we must be emptied. When I reached the end of that first street, whatever I had been full of—self-belief, self-reliance—was drained in an instant. I had nothing to offer. I was all out of good works. I was empty. And that's when God used me, filling me with faith. God blessed that woman with the safe return of her life savings, but I have to admit, I really got the best part of that deal! I left her home feeling richer than I had ever felt in my entire life.

4

The Reluctant Passenger

Wendy McKelvy

My mother and I have always been extremely close and always look forward to spending time together, particularly when that time includes shopping. Back in 1985, I was about to graduate from Arizona State University; what could be better than spending the whole day together shopping for a graduation dress?

It was a clear, beautiful day, made even more exciting by the fact that Mom had turned up in her new sporty little car that I hadn't seen before. Better still, I got to drive.

Those were the days when seat belts were rarely used—in fact, I don't believe I had ever put one on in my entire life. And this day was no different.

We were on a busy three-lane road that led to a major freeway. I pulled up at a stoplight, and we were chatting as usual, waiting for the light to turn green. Completely without warning, the thought popped into my head that we both should put on our seat belts. It was so random and out of the blue that I couldn't easily dismiss it. So I reached down and plugged my belt in.

"Why in the world are you doing that?" asked Mom.

"I don't know," I replied. "I just think we should probably start wearing our seat belts."

She was a little surprised, but she decided to do the same. She struggled with the unfamiliar belt in the new car and couldn't get it to clip in, so she quickly gave up. "It's too much trouble," she said.

I didn't understand why I was doing it, but something compelled me to reach over and help get hers fastened. By the time she was strapped in, the light turned green, and we drove off. Within less than a mile we had accelerated up to fifty miles per hour, and a car turned left across our lane directly in front of us. I had no time to slow down or swerve, and all I could do was yell out that we were about to hit it.

The impact of the fifty-mile-per-hour collision was unbelievably intense. The noise of the impact, the force on our torsos and necks as we were brought to an instant halt, was all too much to take in. And yet our seat belts held us securely in place. Within a few minutes we were free from the car, standing by the side of the road, shocked and full of adrenaline, but very much alive.

Both Mom and I sustained just a couple of cracked ribs, and the people in the other car were unharmed. If we hadn't put on our seat belts, my mom and I both would have gone through the windshield, and there's no way we would have walked away from something like that.

It was so uncharacteristic of me to even think about

using a seat belt, but to have that thought just pop into my head at a stoplight and act on it was truly divine intervention. It was a miracle, a God thing through and through. And as you might imagine, since then I've never had to be reminded to wear my seat belt!

5

Sunflowers and Miracles

Carolyn Hoeflein

Suicide left its mark on my family, and most of us had spent the two years following in a kind of fog. But I gradually noticed that it was changing; I was coming back to life. I slowly moved from someone who believed in God but didn't pursue a relationship with Him, to the kind of Christian who longs for God to act in every part of her day.

It all started when I was lying awake at night, unable to sleep, listening to the radio. I was due to go back to work the next day, and I was not happy about reaching the end of my Christmas break and greeting the changes lying ahead for me at work.

In the very early hours of the morning, I heard a guest tell the radio DJ about something that happened when he had been out driving with his son one night. It all started with the son telling his dad, "I don't believe in miracles."

"Why not?" asked his dad.

"I've never seen one. I don't believe they exist."

"I don't get how you've never seen one," said the dad. "They're all around you."

The son was not convinced. "I just don't believe in them," he said.

"Have you ever asked God for a miracle?" asked the dad.

"Well, no."

"Then ask for one."

"Okay," said the son. "God, send me a miracle!"

"No!" said the dad. "You've got to be more specific."

"Okay, God, send me a miracle *right now*," the son said.

"No, be more specific than that," said the dad. "Ask God to give you a miracle in the next ten miles."

And so he did. The son asked God for a miracle in the next ten miles. When they reached mile nine and a half, the father stopped the car. "Do you see a miracle?" he asked.

"No," said the son.

"Look around. Do you see a miracle?" Again, the son couldn't see anything miraculous around him.

"Look there, on the side of the road," said the dad. "Do you see that sunflower? It's all by itself. There are no fields of sunflowers, yet there it grows on the side of the road. That is a miracle."

I fell asleep soon after that, but the story was still firmly in my mind when I woke up and got ready for work the next day. As I was thinking about the day ahead, I prayed, "God, I need a miracle. I need a really big miracle. I will take anything You've got, but send me a miracle."

With that, I finished getting ready for work and headed off to the campus. Within an hour of arriving at work, we had a meeting, and I was amazed. I had won two door prizes, and a certain supervisor that I had been dreading working with had his start date pushed back three weeks.

I chose not to believe that this was all a coincidence, but a sign that God was listening to me. So I carried on. For a whole month I asked for miracles. Every morning I asked, and throughout the month I saw miracle after miracle. When I was hungry, food appeared. When I was too busy, time appeared, and conversations occurred. I needed to find a second job, and sure enough an opportunity presented itself, and I got the job. Even finding a very small baby squirrel, making sure it stayed alive, and finding a home for it with wildlife rescue staff seemed to me to be yet another miracle.

At the heart of it was a strong feeling that I should share the story I had heard on the radio that night. I told friends, I told acquaintances, I told anyone who would listen, anyone I could. I just felt that there was someone who desperately needed to hear the story so that he or she might ask and receive as well.

One of the people I told was Cindy. Cindy was a lovely young woman, married and desperate to have a baby. Try as they might, she was unable to get pregnant. After months and months of trying and numerous doctor visits, Cindy finally became pregnant, but she miscarried a month later. In her sadness I shared the story as one of hope. She listened, and we often talked about looking for sunflowers on the side of the road or in our daily journeys.

I started to wonder whether it was selfish of me to keep on asking for miracles. Was I getting greedy? I thought I might be, so I stopped, and life returned to normal. Then I saw Cindy again. She told me she was pregnant again and about how she had traveled to see her family in San Antonio and while there had really wanted to visit her grandparents' graves. It made her sad to see the site was unkempt, leaves and sticks all over their graves, and the picture of them that was once mounted under her grandmother's name was gone. Cindy said she must have looked like a madwoman as she thrashed around and dug through the leaves searching for the picture.

She finally found it. She wept by their graves, praying for her unborn child as well as the baby that had died. And she asked for a miracle—a sign that God could hear her. Then, walking along the creek that her grandparents loved, she saw them: three perfect sunflowers, standing all alone.

God finds ways to speak to us. Whether it's when we're trying to get to sleep or when we're actively looking for reassurance, God has ways of speaking to us. And so often, when we pause and listen to God, we discover that He wants to remind us of the plain and simple but life-changing truth: He loves us.

6

A Second Chance

Steve Nestor

There are many words that can make you cringe and wince, but a few can send fear raging through your blood in an instant. When you're sitting at one end of a long, quiet hallway, following what was supposed to be a routine medical examination, and hear the word *cancer*, that's exactly how it feels.

There were more tests to be done, but when the results came back, the news was even worse: "The cancer is in the advanced stages," I was told.

"What are my options?"

"We suggest that now is a good time to get your affairs in order."

Get my affairs in order? I am not a stupid man, but I honestly had no idea what that meant. I had lived most of my life footloose and fancy-free. What affairs could I possibly have to get in order?

Even though they could make no guarantees, they

decided that my care should be aggressive. I was scheduled for surgery the next day, when they would remove the tumors from my neck. Before that, a battery of tests probed every square inch of my body and revealed still more of that dirty word; cancer had invaded other parts of me as if I were a broken-down, unguarded border fence.

As a wanderer, a free bird of sorts, I had let my addictions lead me wherever they wanted. I had lived for pleasure, ignoring any and all consequences of my actions. But now, in a hospital gown surrounded by strangers, I was beginning to question the choices I had made. I was beginning to see the ramifications of a life wasted on pleasure. I could have been the prodigal son, but perhaps it was too late to come home.

As the weeks passed, I became convinced that I was dying. I had good reason, too, as my body began to show signs of decay. Eating became more difficult, and the very smell of food sickened me. I dropped from 195 to 88 pounds in a short period of time. All my hair was gone, and I looked like walking death.

Death wasn't limited to the outside. Death was becoming a constant nightmare as well. I tried to grasp the reality that my life was almost over, but I just could not get past the fact that I had once been a healthy, virile alpha male. I had been strong and determined and not at all easily intimidated, yet I couldn't find that person within me anymore.

As I began to experience all the symptoms and side effects of my treatments, I became angry. And I didn't have a clue why.

Over the course of nine months, I was hospitalized eight times. I had multiple surgeries, almost died twice, and became a familiar face to the emergency room staff. About midway through my treatments my sister took me to her home for some much-needed rest. While there, I picked up a new condition: a severe case of shingles. Once again I was hospitalized; only this time I was in isolation for thirteen days, during most of which I was heavily sedated. The blisters were painful, and the scars they left behind are a constant reminder of this horrific journey.

I eventually returned home, but something else took me down, and I had to be hospitalized again. Doctors gave up, telling me that they had "not seen the progress we had hoped for." Was this the end? Was it all about to be over? I lay in my hospital bed, staring at the door, wondering how much longer I had.

It was late in the afternoon when my doctors entered my room one day. I lifted my head from the pillow of my cranked-up bed. They spoke medical jargon that was beyond me, but in my mind their meaning was clear: "Go home and die."

I lay in the darkness, counting the circles on the ceiling. I started to cry. Somehow I felt calm. Then I heard Him—a voice as clear as your favorite radio station on a star-filled night. *You are not going to die; I have something for you to do.* Coming from a family of pranksters, I first thought someone was standing behind the curtain that had been pulled around my bed. With all the strength I could muster, I yanked the curtain as hard as I could. No one was there. I lay back down and continued counting circles and crying. Then the voice spoke for a second time; only this time it was louder. *You are not going to die.* As I lay in total confusion, I could hear my mother reciting, "Raise them in the way they should go."

The next day, the sun coming through the blinds and my

breakfast untouched on the tray, my mother's pastor entered the room.

"I heard a voice last night, telling me I wasn't going to die and that it had something for me to do. Can you explain it to me?" I was feeling skeptical, and maybe the pastor could tell.

He just stared back at me for a while before saying, "Just follow your heart."

I was discharged later that day. I didn't want to talk to anyone. I just wanted to feel sorry for myself and be quiet. In the moments of silence I knew God was calling me to a life of service. I knew He was calling, but I wasn't giving Him my answer.

Weeks passed; then one day, not knowing how I would respond, my mother knocked quietly on my door. "The doctor wants to see you today. Can you go?"

I was reluctant, but I pulled my frail frame to the edge of the bed and rose gingerly to my feet. It was after hours, and the hallway was dark when we arrived at the hospital. For the next several hours I was put through every imaginable diagnostic test. Once the final X-ray had been taken, the technician said, "Don't leave. The doctor wants to talk with you." I returned to his office and climbed onto the exam table. It felt cold, just as I remembered it.

After an age of waiting the doctor entered the room. I noticed a small grin breaking the left side of his face. In nine months this was the first and only time I had seen this man smile. Then in what seemed like a whisper, he said, "I've got good news." He turned, looked at me, and said, "All the tests came back negative. There is no sign of cancer in your body. This is not medically possible, and I do not understand."

It was my turn to smile. "I think I understand."

I walked into the hallway, found my mom, and told her the good news. She was so shocked she couldn't speak.

My appetite returned almost immediately. Within two weeks I was up to 130 pounds and gaining. I had also returned to my old habits. A late-night visit to my dealer had me back in party mode. I was running faster than ever before—running directly away from God.

A year or more went by in this way. My father lost his own short battle with cancer, and as I sat at the kitchen table, rolling my supply for the day, a burning question seemed to ignite my brain. It was the same God speaking, only this time, silently. *Do you really want to live your life this way?* I thought, *Do I?* No. I did not.

I immediately got up from the table and walked to the bathroom to flush my most recent purchase down the toilet. I knelt beside my bed, trying hard to recall the prayers I had learned as a child. I can remember saying, "I know you are calling me to preach, but I cannot do that, for I am addicted. If you want me to preach, then you will have to take this habit from me." It was as if someone reached down and lifted a five-thousand-pound weight from my shoulders. That day God performed His second miracle; not only had He healed me from stage four Hodgkin's lymphoma, He had now rescued me from my stupidity. For the first time in my life, I was a free man.

A year or so later I found out that on the night I heard God's call and made the choice to follow Him, a lifelong friend of mine had been praying for me. He had been anointed on my behalf, and I believe that his simple act of faith changed everything for me.

That was all twenty years ago, and I remain free from both cancer and my addictions. My greatest joy is my service to God, and He has enabled me to accomplish more than I ever dreamed. I am indeed a walking, talking miracle all because God chose to give me a second chance.

7

Miracle Glasses

Tammy Neal

In the early '90s, my husband attended Appalachian Bible College in Beckley, West Virginia. The college is about one hundred miles from our home, and each Monday he'd get in the car and drive off for the week of study before returning home on Friday. His eyesight wasn't great, so he had to wear either glasses or contacts in order to be able to see well enough to drive.

Those were the days when contacts were expensive and you really only ever had one pair. His old glasses were broken, and his prescription needed updating, so he did not have anything other than his contacts. We knew it was time for him to go to an eye doctor, but with our finances being what they were, we just couldn't afford it.

One weekend while he was home, one of his contacts broke, and we didn't have enough money to replace the contacts or the glasses. We prayed about the situation, but there didn't seem to be any solution. If I drove him back to Beckley, he wouldn't have been able to see the board in the classroom. The only idea we could come up with was for him not to go back to school until we were able to pull enough money together for an eye appointment and new lenses or glasses. It wasn't much of an option.

We were in Teays Valley at the time, out on Route 34. It's a heavily traveled area, and for around here, a four-lane highway with a turn lane is fairly large. The sky was clear that day, and as we drove along, with traffic busy as usual and me at the wheel, my husband twisted around in his seat. "Pull over," he said. "I think I just saw something." I hadn't seen anything, so I was sure that he hadn't either, but I did what he asked and slowed down at the side of the road.

He jumped out and walked back a little way before stepping out into the middle of the road. I watched him bend down, pick something up, and examine it in his hands. It was a pair of glasses. He put them on, smiled, and walked back to me. "I can see!" he said triumphantly.

That pair of old glasses was a close enough match for him to be able to use them. He could drive again and was able to go back to college and continue the year, all the time wearing his miracle glasses. And by the time we were able to afford a visit to an eye doctor, several years had passed, and those miracle glasses were still just as good as the day he picked them up off the highway. God provided for my husband's need for glasses in a mighty way, just as He always does.

8

The Siege

Maggie Duncan

"Help! Help! They're trying to kill me!"

Maybe I thought he was dreaming. Maybe I thought it was a joke. Maybe I thought *I* was dreaming. Whatever the confusion at first, it didn't take long for the residue of sleep to get flushed out of my system as the adrenaline took over. Fear woke me up faster than a bullet as I listened in the darkness.

"Let me in! They're trying to kill me!"

This was no dream. I was in Haiti, in an apartment along with thirteen other Americans, near a little village called Coupon, just outside Port-au-Prince. We were half a mile away from any neighbors, two stories up in an otherwise empty apartment block, and had been helping the local church run a crusade the previous week. It had been a great week, and we had seen God do amazing things in people's lives, but whatever was going on outside the apartment right now was totally unexpected.

As usual we had all gone to bed at eleven thirty that Thursday night—an hour after the electricity in the area had been turned off. We were all tired from the day's hard work but so happy with the way the meetings had been going. The other four women and I slept at one end of the apartment, with all but one of the guys sleeping at the other end.

Bruce, whom we called Mr. Haiti, was the most seasoned missionary in our group. Over the last several years he had made three or four trips to this village annually, and he was very well-known by everyone. Because he was so comfortable there, he preferred to sleep outside on a mattress on the back balcony. It was from there that I could hear him shouting.

As I ran from my bed, I knew that it was his voice calling out in the darkness. Once I was in the kitchen, I could see Bruce banging on the window, his face lit up by flashlights shining erratically behind him.

In an instant Jason, our group leader, was in the kitchen, opening the heavy steel door onto the balcony. He reached into the darkness and grabbed Bruce, desperately trying to pull him in to safety. But Bruce's hands had been bound up with zip ties, and his attackers were holding on to him, using him as bait.

I have no idea how Jason won that struggle, but somehow—thanks, I'm sure, to some Holy Spirit–induced strength—he managed to wrestle Bruce away and into the apartment. But he was unable to close the door behind him; the attackers had wedged a piece of wood in the doorway, keeping it open just enough for them to roll out the next phase of their attack. I watched in horror as, through the gap in the door and through freshly broken kitchen windows, their guns emerged and started firing.

I ran along with the other women back to our bedroom. We huddled behind the beds and prayed. What else could we do?

Our men fought off the attackers with their strength. We had no electricity, no weapons, and no contact with the outside world. The nearest house was too far away to be of any immediate help, and as we prayed, we guessed that it would be only a matter of time before the gunmen killed our defenseless men, forced their way into the apartment, and came to get us.

Staccato gunfire blended with the shouts and screams of our good friends. We heard them plead with the attackers to stop shooting, commanding them in the name of Jesus to stop, but the firing continued. Still we prayed. Gradually I came to the realization that I was going to die. This was the moment; this was the place. After fifty years on this earth, I would soon be leaving my husband, four daughters, and two grandsons behind. Soon I would be in heaven.

I prayed for peace as I've never prayed for anything before. At once I felt the hand of Christ on my shoulder, giving me the peace for which I asked. I felt ready. I prayed for God to protect my family, take care of my grandchildren, and give my husband peace in my death. I was ready to be with Jesus. I just hoped that they would shoot me somewhere that would make the journey quick. So I prayed some more, listening to the shooting and the screaming for another thirty minutes.

And then it stopped.

I could hear Bruce yelling again; only this time he was

telling us that it was safe to come out and that we should bring blankets with us because there was so much blood and they needed help. Leaving the bedroom, I saw the damage for myself as the injured men were scattered throughout the apartment. Rex was on the back balcony with Brad holding his leg like a tourniquet, screaming for a belt or something. Morgan had been carried to a back bedroom, bleeding from his leg. Bruce had been shot clean through his elbow, and he was wandering around shouting combat orders to everyone. Chris was lying on the floor with his hand wrapped in a towel. We scurried around in the darkness, trying to help, listening to the shouts and moans.

Jason had jumped out his back bedroom window to the side of the apartment building. He had jammed both of his ankles on the twenty-foot fall but still managed to run a half-mile, cross an eight-foot moat, and scale a twelve-foot metal gate to reach the nearest house and get help from the local missionary. They had returned, fired a gun into the air, shouted that the police were there too (one lie they wouldn't need to repent of!), and watched the six armed attackers run off into a field and disappear.

That night, after we were escorted to the missionary's home, over thirty Haitian men from the village of Coupon encircled the house. They stayed there all night, protecting us in the darkness. And when daylight finally came and we felt safe to leave, we went back to the apartment to gather our things. As we were walking there, several of the Haitians from the village lined the road, nothing but sorrow displayed on their faces. They were broken and ashamed, and many of them hugged us and apologized.

Their spirit touched us, but we still decided to leave the country immediately. We somehow overcame the bureaucracy that regulates arrivals and departures on the island, and by that evening—just twelve hours after the attack had begun—we were on our way to the airport, sharing in the tears and the prayers of the local church members we were leaving behind.

The year following the attack was very difficult for me. Fear would grip me whenever I encountered a situation where I felt out of control. Others in the group felt the same, and we each had therapy with a specialist who dealt with post-traumatic stress disorder. But I never wavered in my faith. I knew it was a process for me to work through, and through it all God has remained faithful.

I have been able to stay in touch with some of the children we ministered to and hope to go back someday. For now, though, I take pleasure in the fact that our church is building a school, just a few hours from Coupon, that will continue the work we began.

And I also know this: never in all my life have I felt such peace as I did on the night I was convinced that I was about to die. I felt so loved by God, so forgiven, so close to Him, and while I never want to go through that experience again, I'm blessed to have known what it is to be loved by God so completely. Today, two years after that wild night, I know it has drawn me much closer to the Lord. I want everyone to know what it is to share such feelings of peace and love.

9

He Watches Over Me

Cheryl Thompson

Nobody told me to hop onto the trunk of the car as it pulled away from my house. It was all my own doing. I was seventeen years old, liked to have fun, and had never given a thought to dying. Why wouldn't I jump onto the back of the silver 1976 Ford Granada as my friends eased it out onto the road?

Even thirty-five years later I still remember how fun it felt to be holding on to the trunk as we sailed down the road that evening. I remember my friends on the inside of the vehicle cheering me on. But my memories are scrambled when I try recalling what happened once the car started making a turn so they could take me back home.

I can't imagine the fear my mom felt as she stood outside our house, watching her teenage daughter disappear from view and the car slam to a halt. She ran down to find me lying in the ditch on the side of the road. Apparently I had gotten up and run to the ditch after falling off the trunk, and

I was screaming at her about having a terrible headache but that there was no way I was going to let anyone take me to the hospital. After that, Mom told me, I passed out.

By the time the ambulance got me to the hospital, the prayer chain had kicked in, and word of my injury had reached almost everybody in our church. There were friends waiting beyond the automatic doors, praying continuously. And they needed to, for as the doctors delivered their initial assessment to my parents, the news was not good. They told them that my pupils were fixed and dilated, indicating that the injury was so severe that even if I did survive, there was little chance I would ever be able to function for myself.

They ran a CT scan, which revealed I had a blood clot between my brain and my skull. The clot was large and pushing up against my brain, which had moved by as much as a couple of inches. And then, just as they repeated the scan, the clot disappeared. It vanished completely. My lifeless eyes returned to normal. The doctors were amazed, telling my parents they had no way of explaining why it had happened. But Mom and Dad knew, just as everyone else knew who was praying that day.

Throughout the weekend I was kept in the ICU, where they monitored me, before letting me stay in another part of the hospital for most of the following week. When another CT scan revealed that my brain had moved back to its original position, they let me go home.

I don't remember much of the week at all, but even today I still have not recovered my sense of smell. I don't mind much; in fact, I see it as a constant reminder of what God can do and how fortunate I was that He allowed a physical miracle to happen in my life.

But the story doesn't end there. About a week after I left the hospital, I visited a small convenience store near my home. The clerk was glad to see me back and wanted to tell me a story about something else that had happened on the night of my accident. A woman had come into the store, visibly shaken. She told the clerk that she had almost run over a girl who had fallen off the back of a car. She was convinced that she would have hit her had the girl not jumped up and run into the ditch at the side of the road.

I have no memory of the accident, and certainly no memory of getting up and running to safety. But I know this one thing for sure: God was faithfully watching over me that day. No one can tell me otherwise!

10

The School Bill

Christine Pringle-Shreve

I was a freshman, preparing to start my third trimester at Bible college. I was used to working hard—not just carrying full-time units but working two jobs to help pay for my tuition and expenses. Even so, I was still in debt.

Things got worse when my parents told me they couldn't help me financially at that time. Final payments were due the following Monday, and without full payment, I would not be allowed to register. Dropping out seemed to be my only option, but how could that be right? I was so sure that I was meant to be at that particular school at that particular time.

With just three days to go before the payment deadline, I went to see the school's president and asked for his advice. Patiently he listened to my heavy heart, then said, "Let's pray." It was not an earthshaking prayer, though I remember him asking God to release funds in my direction. While he prayed with confidence, I prayed with timidity.

I walked straight out of the meeting with the president and was told that there was a message for me at the registrar's office. It was a short message but one that still amazes me today.

Christine, Pastor Haynes phoned to say that he and his wife have been praying and feel the Lord asking them to send money towards your college finances. They want to give 90 percent of your fees.

Pastor Haynes was the man who had dedicated me as a baby, eighteen years earlier. It amazed me that he and his wife had decided to give me the money on the morning I visited the college president and that they had phoned to confirm I was at the school and made their offer at the very moment I was in the meeting, praying that simple prayer. God knows what we need before we need it, and His timing is remarkable. I was amazed and grateful in equal measure.

But there was another surprise waiting for me when I returned to my dorm. In that day's mail was a check from a member of my home church with a note to say that just a few days earlier the Lord had directed her to send me this gift. I checked: it was the exact amount I needed to pay the remainder of my school bill.

All that weekend I was stunned by the generosity of friends and the love and provision of God. And on Monday morning, I registered for my next year of college, excited about whatever else God might have in store for me.

11

A Letter to Baby Alex

Shannon Edds

This is not your typical miracle story. There is no healing in it, no miraculous recovery that defies medical understanding. There's just a precious moment in an unborn baby's life that I will cherish for the rest of my life.

In February 2012, I found out that I was pregnant. My husband and I already had three precious boys, and as we sat through the eight-week scan, I felt a familiar sense of relief as we saw and heard the beating of a tiny heart.

Since I was thirty-six at the time, I asked if I should see a high-risk doctor just to make sure everything was okay. It was mid-April by the time we had the appointment, and since the scan looked good, I hardly gave the finger-stick blood test a second thought.

April 26 changed all that. The results from the test came back, and they left me in shock. Our baby had a 1 in 24 chance of Downs and a 1 in 7 chance of Trisomy 18. I found it hard to believe, but I did not lose heart. Surely there had been a mistake. Wouldn't the next checkup put things right again?

But the next time we sat in the darkened room while the ultrasound went to work, it only confirmed the worst. My baby was measuring a week behind typical growth—something none of my other babies had done—and my baby's legs were crossed, which I had discovered in my research was a sign of Trisomy 18. Yet somehow not all was lost, and we were still optimistic when we went for a further scan at fifteen weeks. We were having a little baby boy! How great was that?

A further scan at sixteen and a half weeks revealed that there was a problem with the baby's heart; instead of the usual four chambers, our little baby boy had just two. Through the tears we asked if we should go see a prenatal cardiologist to see what could be done to save our baby boy. Our doctor told us that he first wanted to perform an amniocentesis to determine whether our baby had a chromosomal defect. "If there is a chromosomal defect," he said, "there will be no need to go to a cardiologist."

I lay there, desperately trying not to cry as he guided the needle into my uterus. I looked at my baby boy on the ultrasound, watching him move smartly away from the needle, his instincts causing him to retreat from harm.

It took eleven long days for the results to come back. It was as we had feared: our son had Trisomy 18. Knowing most babies with Trisomy 18 are stillborn or live just a few hours after birth, I asked the doctor, "How long do you think he will survive?"

"Most babies live only thirty-two to thirty-four weeks while they're still in the womb," he said.

We were completely devastated. I was eighteen weeks pregnant at that point, and over the next few months, we came to cherish every moment we had with our baby.

We decided to name him Alex Michael, and the boys called him Baby Alex as they hugged and kissed him and told him "good night" through my belly. I played music for him and held him by wrapping my arms around my very pregnant belly, hoping he could feel loved. I bought two special monogrammed blankets and two special gowns for Alex: one set for hospital pictures, and then to keep, and one set to bury him with. No one should ever have to shop for an unborn baby's burial clothes.

We took a special family beach trip at the end of July and took photos on the beach. My favorite one shows me standing at the edge of the ocean, holding my belly, with Alex's name written in the sand beside me. As soon as the photo was taken, an ocean wave gently rolled onto the shore and washed Alex's name away. I cried then. I knew Alex would not be with us much longer.

As we approached the start of the final trimester, I knew that God was preparing my heart for what was to come. Regular checks reassured us that Alex was still alive and that his heart was beating, but I knew he was getting tired. After one scan I pushed on my belly to see if I could get Alex to move. He pushed back on my hand! He did this three times in a row, and I was so glad I could still feel him move.

That was the last time I felt him move. On the night of August 21, 2012, I went to sleep, unaware that the miracle was about to happen. I woke up at about 3:00 a.m., instantly aware that God was filling my mind with words that I had to write down. Crying as I did so, I poured the words onto the page, watching as a letter to our precious Alex was revealed in front of me.

I knew he was gone. I knew it that night, and I knew it as we went for our planned checkup the next day. And all through the final ultrasound, the labor, and birth the following day, I knew that God had woken me up so that I was awake the moment our baby boy slipped away.

No mother should have to give birth to her child who makes no sound and who is perfectly still throughout. But in the pain of that experience—just as in the pain of the grieving that continued through the months that followed—I am always brought back to the night that God allowed me to experience Alex slipping away. It comforts me that I was able to be aware of that precious moment in my baby's life. I thank God for waking me up that night, for the miracle that will forever comfort me until the moment I am reunited with my precious son, Alex. I thank God for the thirty weeks that He allowed us to get to know and love baby Alex . . . and for these words:

God lent you to us for just a little while.
We never got to hear your cry.
We never got to see your smile.
You left this world as quietly as you came,
And touched our lives with the brush of your angel
   wings.
How beautiful you are Baby Alex,
And now forever will be!
We know that Jesus is holding you, rocking you,
   loving you.

When we get there, we will hold you, rock you,
   love you—
But for now, Jesus will take our place.
The angels are singing you lullabies—
And how beautiful that must be!
God lent you to us for just a little while.
And, for that, we are thankful.
For we got to know a little angel named Alex
   Michael.
And our lives will forever be changed.

   We love you, Alex.

12

The Voice

Jamey Smith

They say that we start storing permanent memories sometime around three or four years of age. How and why those earliest recollections are created is still a bit of a mystery for many but not for me. I know exactly why my brain wanted to make sure I would never forget my first memory—because it was formed on the day I almost died.

I was at my first pool party. I was toddling around on my three-and-a-half-year-old legs, running up and down by the pool, watching the other older kids splashing, swimming, and having fun. It looked exciting in there, but I knew that the pool was dangerous for me. To my little eyes it seemed as big as an ocean, and I knew to stay away.

But even though the pool was off-limits, nothing was going to stop me from finding out what was going on around it. I wove my way between the giant legs of adults dangling from chairs and draped over sun loungers. I peeked behind mountains of towels. I squeezed between tables. But it wasn't until I made it to the edge of the pool that I found something truly memorable: there in front of me was a small pool, just to the side of the main one. It was perfect for me—round like a ball, as small as a car, and with beautiful bubbles dancing around in the water.

I jumped right in. The heat of the water took me by surprise, but that was nothing compared to the shock of finding out that this pool was far too deep for me. I remember sinking down as the bubbles passed by me on their way up.

Just as the water looked as though it was fogging up all around me, an incredible sense of peace settled over me. And then, clear as anything, I heard a voice. It was calm, motherly. I knew that I could trust her.

"Jamey," she said calmly. "Put your hand up, Jamey." I guess I didn't do what she said straightaway, for again she said, "Jamey, put your hand up." This time I lifted it up high. The air felt cold on my fingers as they waved above the surface.

The next thing I knew I was being pulled up out of the water, high into the air, and straight into the arms of my mother. She was in hysterics. Me? I was still calm, wondering what had just happened, still in awe of the beautiful voice I had heard in the water. I wondered why Mom was so freaked out when something so great had just happened.

Thirty years have passed since I was hauled out of the Jacuzzi, and the memories are just as strong today as they ever were. But it took years before I could understand more clearly what went on as I sank toward the bottom; it was a God thing, through and through.

13

A Path to Healing

Donna Crum

The accident happened in 2003. It was inventory time in the grocery store where I worked, and even though I had a feeling that I should not go into the freezer by myself, I ignored it and carried on. I was pulling out one of the steel transits when a wheel got trapped, and the whole thing fell onto me—289 pounds of frozen turkey packed into a metal container. It hit me on the head, and the damage it inflicted was extensive: chronic pain, back spasms, nerve root damage on my sciatic nerve, and a herniated and bulging disc. My short-term memory suffered, and I developed carpal tunnel syndrome in my forearms. I was seen by at least ten different doctors, including one of the top neurosurgeons in California, and sat through two CT scans and eight MRIs. Every specialist told me the same thing: my condition was inoperable. All I could do was live with it.

But living with my condition didn't always mean I felt

that I was really living. I have been through some difficult times since the accident. I was hooked on the pain and anti-spasm meds, and I turned to alcohol in search of relief. The pain eventually got so bad that I even started to wonder whether death might be the only source of relief, so I tried to kill myself with booze and pills.

At the heart of it all was the fact that I was mad at God. The constant repetition of waking up in pain, enduring the day in pain, and going to bed in pain gradually turned me into more and more of a mess.

By 2012, I was no longer quite so angry at God, and I had even started going back to church, but the pain was still with me, so I decided to change doctors again. My new doctor wanted to run a new MRI just to see what was still causing my pain, and she told me that it would take about a month for the appointment to come through. I am claustrophobic and didn't much like the idea of another MRI, so the long delay was fine by me. But when the hospital called me the next day and told me that the MRI was scheduled for that day, I felt the old nerves return. With much prayer and grit-ted teeth, I managed to get through it okay.

I waited the usual two weeks for the call from the doctor's office telling me that the results were in. Only this time the results were different. This time the scan revealed no damage to my discs and spine. "According to the MRI, there's noth-ing wrong with your back," the doctor said.

"This is a joke, right?" I said.

"No. Apart from minimal arthritis, you have a healthy spine."

"Well, there must have been a mix-up with the results," I

said, adding that I would bring my previous test results with me to my appointment in three days' time.

At my appointment, while sitting inside the consulting room and waiting for the doctor to arrive, I was nervous. I had the stack of MRI films with me—images that revealed how messed up my back was—but I knew that the latest tests were correct. I knew I had been healed, and I knew how it happened. How was I going to tell her that the Lord healed my back? And why did I still feel pain?

I listened as she looked through the charts outside my room. I could hear the sound of the thick sheets being turned over as she puzzled over the two opposing results.

"This can't be," the doctor said before resuming her examination. "Well . . . anything is possible." She came into my room. "I don't understand; there's no sign of that major damage anymore. I'm going to call the MRI technician to see if they can help make sense of it."

I knew it was my turn to speak. "I know why."

"Oh really?"

"Yes," I said, tears filling my eyes. "Jesus healed my back when I started going back to church last October. My back was anointed with holy oil, and people prayed for the Lord to heal my back. And look . . . He did!"

She paused for a moment. She was crying too.

Over the course of a few weeks, the doctor finally got to the bottom of it all. My back really had been healed, just as her test had revealed, but there was a reason for the continued pain: I have multiple sclerosis. Without my back being healed, the MS would have gone undetected and untreated, its symptoms masked by the injury that everyone said was inoperable. Now, since the doctors know that my back isn't the problem, they can treat what really ails me and stop the progress of this disease.

I am finally able to live my life with no pain at all on some days. On days when I still have chronic pain, I am able to manage and use the drugs well without abusing them. And who knows—the Lord might heal this latest condition as well. I don't know whether He will, but I do know that I can accept whatever His will is. And I know that He has healed my spine and restored my faith in Him, and my life will never be the same.

I share my story with so many people I meet, including a new wave of doctors who are treating the MS. Some look at me as though I am crazy and delusional, but my husband goes with me and tells them that every word of my story is true. And maybe my MRIs will help those who don't believe to start rethinking what God can do and how He might be able to change their lives as well. That's what I'm praying for.

14

Faithful Provider

Libby Hill

I come from a missionary family. We're used to living by faith, but when we moved back to the States in 2011, things weren't easy for us. We had been away in China for nine years, and my dad couldn't get a job. We were trying simply to get by, living in an RV loaned to us by a friend and spending as little money as possible.

We fished in the little ponds available to the residents of the RV park and had stocked up on staples like peanut butter and tuna. But eventually the propane that we used to heat, cool, and cook ran low, and we couldn't afford to fill it up. We didn't know what to do.

Finally one day the propane in the RV ran out completely. We went to bed with the tanks showing empty, but when we woke up the next morning and tried the stove, it worked. The heating worked, too, and when the weather got hot, we were able to cool the RV as well.

It carried on like this, with the tanks having enough fuel for each day and the ponds offering up enough fish to keep us going. Between the tanks and the ponds, they were our daily bread. Not until God had provided a new place for us to stay and the money to refill the RV with propane did the ponds stop teeming with fish and the stove refuse to come on.

God is good. Miracles are real still today.

15

I Don't Believe in Coincidences

Angie Williams

For some reason I felt I needed to update my Facebook status on that particular Sunday morning. I knew it was somehow important to share the words that God was highlighting for me that day:

"Joshua 24:15: 'But as for me and my household, we will serve the LORD' (NIV). If you don't have a personal relationship with Christ, I pray you will find Him today."

Once we had gotten home from church and eaten lunch, my husband went to work, and the girls and I took an afternoon nap. A little after 5:00 p.m., the three of us woke up, and I started to do dishes and get dinner ready. With Averie, our seven-month-old, playing in a standing bouncer seat, and Adley, our two-year-old, watching a movie, it was one of those afternoons where time doesn't seem to matter.

At 5:20 p.m. my husband called. He wanted to know if we were watching the weather. I switched the TV channel and saw the satellite images of a violent storm. It was heading north of us, so we decided that the girls and I were safe. We hung up, and I got back to preparing the food.

Then my mom called from Kansas City. She wondered if we knew about the tornado warning and was checking that we were okay. I told her that we were fine, that we were watching the Weather Channel, and it was nothing to worry about. After all, down in Joplin we get a lot of tornado warnings.

Then the sirens started going off. I took the girls to the bathroom, and we all sat in the tub and waited. The sirens stopped, we climbed out of the bathtub, and we went back to doing whatever we had been doing.

Mom called again. She wanted me to check on the weather, and I looked out of the window as we spoke. Maybe she was right to be a little worried; the sky was darker than I had ever seen it before at that time of the day. The TV told me that the storm was right over the heart of Joplin, but to the east the sky was a pretty, light blue. How bad could it be?

"Mom, I think it's okay. There's a little hail coming down out front, but the darker—"

"It's hailing? That's not a good sign. Get in the hallway, Angie."

I got the girls together, put Averie in her baby walker, and then gathered some pillows, Adley's special blanket, and a toy doggie that she just can't sleep without. I turned down the TV so I could better hear the noise from outside, shut as many doors as I could, and followed Adley to a spot in the hallway to sit down with my girls. Something didn't feel right, so I took Averie out of her walker, put it back in the other room, and sat back down in the hall. All was calm as we sat there, and I continued talking to my mom the whole time, giving her a play-by-play. But then, in a matter of seconds, the storm turned up.

"Mom, the hail is hitting the front of the house really strong now. It's—" The power went off. I shrieked. It came back on for an instant, then back off for good. And then, with my ears popping from the increased air pressure, I heard the sound—unmistakable, unforgettable.

"Mom, it sounds like there's a train right outside."

"That's it, Angie. Cover your heads and get as low as you can! *Get low!*"

I heard the sound of breaking glass from the light fixtures, followed by the sound of breaking windows. Somehow it still wasn't registering in my mind that there was a tornado coming toward my house. I still thought that the blue skies I had seen meant we were at the edge of the storm. In reality, we were right in its path.

I felt the force of the storm attack the house. It grew stronger and stronger. Then, without warning, the sound of tearing filled my ears. I could feel the wind all over my back and body. The pillow I was holding over my head was ripped out of my hands, and I forced myself even lower down to the ground, gathering the girls even closer to me.

God, please keep us safe! Please put Your angels all around us!

As the tornado tore around us, I wondered what it would be like to wake up in heaven. Would I know that I had died? Would it hurt? I begged God to make it stop, to just make this noise and this wind and violence go away.

It stopped. The wind slowed down, and I checked on the girls. Curled up under my chest, held in by my arms, they had made it safely through. I heard someone calling my name, but the voice sounded small and far-off. It was my mom, still on the phone, which was now buried under some debris nearby. She had heard everything and had no idea whether we made it through or not.

"Mom," I said, after finding the phone and beginning to look around me, "everything's gone."

It was so surreal. It felt like a dream, one in which you feel the most helpless you have ever felt. The rain had started, and huge drops were falling on the three of us. I found one of my husband's coats nearby and threw it over the girls. Then we sat there, in the middle of our destroyed home. *What do I do now?*

I decided that I needed to get the girls to safety. The lightning was striking extremely close, and the rain was coming down hard, so I picked up both girls and carried them past the walls that were no longer there. I wanted to get to where I could be seen by people who would be out trying to help, so I picked my way, barefoot, toward the church a couple of blocks away. The rain was pouring down, and we were cold and wet, but Adley helped shield Averie's face from the rain with her hand. My girls were so brave all along, and I am still so proud of them. As we walked, I didn't look around much; I was too afraid of what I would see. But whenever I did take my eyes off the few feet in front of me, everything was gone.

It was hard to make sense of where we were, and I was far more disoriented than I had ever been. Nothing was recognizable anymore; nothing made sense. As I walked, I heard screams and cries, and my heart broke knowing there were injured and trapped people out there, but I had to keep walking. I had to keep my girls safe.

I held my girls tight as we sat in the deserted parking lot of the church. Just like everywhere else, the church building had been replaced by a pile of timber and dirt, and in the rain and the cold, the fear started to rise within me. I had gotten us as far as I could. There was nothing else I could do.

In time, kind strangers found us and gave us towels and blankets, and we were taken to my mother-in-law's house. We got word to everyone that we were safe and then spent the night together as a family, listening to the rain outside.

In no time at all we began receiving even more kindness and support from our friends and family. There were donations of clothes, household items, toys, and money. We learned how the precise spot in the hall that God had led Adley to sit in was the perfect place for surviving the storm. Her dresser in the next room had tipped to a forty-five-degree angle and was the only thing holding the bricks up and preventing them from crashing down on us. Had Adley chosen to sit a few feet further in either direction, I don't think we would have made it.

I had started that day quoting Scripture and thinking about serving the Lord. I ended it knowing with even greater assurance than ever that putting our trust in Him is the best thing we can ever do.

16

God Always Wins!

Ella Brunt

July 2, 1997. It was supposed to be a family outing on a sail-boat, a perfect way to pass the time on a hot, windy afternoon on Clear Lake at Nassau Bay, Texas. It turned into a tragedy. But it didn't stay that way.

My nephew, Wallace, had offered to take me and my two children out on his eighteen-foot sailboat. Brittany was eight at the time, and my son, Cody, was six, and we all climbed happily aboard, my kids moving a little clumsily in their life jackets. The wind was making it hard for Wallace to launch away from the dock, so both children were told to stay up in the front of the boat while a friendly boater towed us fifty feet off the dock area. We all looked back to wave at the family members standing in the parking lot, watching our family adventure unfold.

Wallace was getting the tacking sail up when a big gust of wind hit us, pushing the boat over on its side as if it were a toy. As we were about to be thrown into the water, Wallace thrust Brittany into my arms. I looked to see Cody at the other end of the boat, his arms stretched out to me in desperation, his eyes wide with fear. The sail came down, hiding him from view. The boat capsized.

I was holding on to Brittany as we floated in the water beside the upturned boat. Wallace had immediately dived under to retrieve Cody. There was no noise that I was aware of, only silence. Wallace shot his head up out of the water, gasped, and disappeared again. Silence again. A few more seconds passed, and Wallace returned, gasped, and disappeared. With each following attempt, he returned alone. Brittany and I began to pray, calling on God to help, crying out to Him for rescue. When Wallace came up the next time, he paused. "Noooo!" he yelled.

"Keep trying!" I screamed before he went back beneath the surface. The silence returned, and I was oblivious to my family on the dock. I was oblivious to everything but my daughter in my arms and my son trapped somewhere beneath the boat. I wanted to dive down, but there was no way I was letting go of Brittany. I knew that I had one simple choice to make: panic or trust God.

Someone on a Jet Ski came by. Calmly I gave Brittany to her and asked her to go get help because my son was under the boat. As she turned back toward the dock, I realized that somehow I felt perfectly peaceful. I forced as much air as I could into my lungs and swam down beneath the boat, praying as I went. I prayed against death, against disabilities, handicaps, and brain damage for Cody. I even began to pray that whatever treatment and medication was going to be given to him, it would do him only good and not harm. Things were so far out of my control; all I could do was surrender to God.

I forced my way down beneath the boat. It was dark down there, and my hands were reaching out for anything they could get a hold of. I felt something that looked like clothing and pulled it closer to see, but it was just the blue casing for one of the sails. I was running out of time, my lungs sending a searing pain through my chest.

When I returned to the surface, I knew that Cody was dead; too much time had passed for him to survive, and I knew that we needed to find his body. Since Jesus raised people from the dead in the Bible, I believed that He could and would do it for us.

At least seven—maybe as many as ten—minutes or more had passed by the time more help came. As the two Jet Skis arrived, Wallace finally made it back to the surface with Cody's limp, blue body. I watched Cody bend backward ninety degrees as he lay across Wallace's shoulder. His life jacket was still tangled in ropes and rigging, and the two men helped untangle him before lifting him onto one of the Jet Skis. The Jet Ski wouldn't start, but by now the boater who had towed us out had come back from across the lake and was offering help. They lifted Cody's body up onto the boat, and we all climbed on, headed for the dock. Cody had no heartbeat. He wasn't breathing. Once again, silence covered everything.

On the way back to the dock, Wallace and the rescuer (an off-duty policeman) began to administer CPR. I bent over him, praying constantly, saying, "I command life to come back into you, in the name of Jesus." A gush of water came out of Cody's mouth; the recovery operation was on. We arrived at the dock, where paramedics took over. I looked at the news helicopters hovering above us. Those vultures upset me, but they were documenting and videotaping Cody's rescue.

Cody was airlifted to Hermann Hospital in Houston, and as my brother drove me there, I called and left a message for my husband, Ted, who was on his way back from work. I spoke with my pastor as we pushed our way through the rush-hour traffic, praying for Cody's life.

Ted was already there when we arrived at the hospital. I ran up to him in relief and held tight to his neck. "Here's the game plan," he said. "We're only going to speak faith-filled words. We're going to believe that Cody will walk out of this hospital 100 percent well. And only people who can agree to that will be allowed around him."

A doctor introduced himself and explained Cody's condition. It was hard to hear the list of problems that our son was facing: irreversible brain damage due to lack of oxygen, lungs that were a total whiteout on X-rays and were bleeding uncontrollably, no pain reflex, the anticipation of brain swelling, and the need for corrective surgery. Cody was in a coma and relying on life-support systems. "I'm afraid I can give you only a one percent chance that your son will ever recover, and if he does survive, he will be in a vegetative state and would need to be institutionalized," he said.

Those words may have entered our ears, but they did not penetrate our hearts. Cody was being treated in the emergency room at that time and would have to be transferred to the PICU before we could see him. As we waited in a side room, away from the news media and journalists who had gathered to cover the story, friends came and joined us. We shared the game plan with them, asking them to join us in believing in a full recovery. Time moved slowly.

Eventually we were told that we could see Cody. A doctor escorted us to the PICU, reminding us of the dire situation as we went. Again the words sounded real, but we refused to let them be the ones we believed. And as we rounded the corner upstairs, we saw twenty of our friends from church gathered outside the PICU, already praying on our behalf.

Before we entered the room, Ted asked, "Can we have some friends and family come in with us to pray over Cody?"

The doctor let them all in, and we crowded around our son's bed, on a mission to pray life into his little body. He looked small in the big bed, dwarfed by the mass of tubes, IVs, the ventilator, and a whole load of other machines. It was a life-or-death situation, and we were choosing life.

Cody was not expected to live through the night. "We've done all we can," said the doctors. "Now all we can do is wait."

So we waited. All night we waited, and when the morning came, Cody was still with us. We watched, waited, and prayed throughout the next day as well, and still he was with us. We placed a picture above his bed—a beautiful photo of Cody, looking healthy and strong. So many times we looked at it and reminded ourselves that this was what we were believing in: total recovery.

There were so many hurdles to overcome: pneumonia, infections, low blood pressure, high fever, cold and turning in of extremities, bedsores. As the days passed by, Cody went through them all, constantly monitored with EEGs, CT scans, and more. Yet we guarded our hearts and continued to believe in a miracle. We played Christian music and teaching tapes on a little tape player we placed on his pillow. We were doing all we knew to do and were trusting God to do what we could not. Ted and I alternated shifts with our son, and at the changeover times we met in the hospital chapel to pray, sing, and have church together. We reminded ourselves that nothing is impossible with God.

I started answering the phone by saying, "Miracle in motion, Cody's mom . . . ," and our hearts were never more set on victory. Of course the doctors thought we were in denial, and they were right. We denied the right for those symptoms to stay with our son.

It took nine and a half days before we saw any sign of improvement in Cody. They took him off the ventilator, and we were amazed to hear that he was breathing on his own. But even this great news came with stern warnings from the doctors. We were not allowed to see him after he was extubated until the next morning. Several days later, when he was transferred to a private room, Cody had to be restrained to the bed. He had started thrashing around and was becoming violent. It was heartbreaking to see this and hear that his change from the gentle boy we knew was due to the brain damage he had sustained. Again we prayed, believing that God had gotten him this far in his recovery and He would complete the work He started. Ted and I believed in total restoration.

Gradually Cody calmed and returned to his normal self. He was transferred to a rehabilitation hospital for a period of therapy that would last anywhere from four to six weeks. Ten days after Cody arrived, he was dismissed. We took him back to Hermann Hospital, where Cody walked back into the PICU, just as we prayed he would. And when Cody introduced himself to the doctors and nurses who had taken care of him, they stood in amazement at his recovery.

On Cody's first Sunday back at church, our pastor asked Cody to join him up front. "Is there anything you'd like to say?"

Cody, our six-year-old miracle child, thought for a second. "Yes," he replied. "God always wins!"

Today Cody is an honor college graduate (University of Texas, summa cum laude) and works in a hospital setting, helping others. He is our miracle in motion. His lungs and his brain were damaged beyond what the doctors believed was reparable, but God knew otherwise. Why? Because as Cody said, God always wins!

Just recently Cody has started sharing what happened to him when he was under the boat. While we were panicking and trying to rescue him, Cody was enjoying the wonders of heaven. But that's another story for another book.

17

A Sale to Remember

Pamela Emmett

I know that Christmas is not about Santa or gifts under the tree, but as a mom of a four-year-old son who only wants a Star Wars X-Wing Starfighter, it's kind of hard not to feel the pressure—especially when money is tight.

That was how life was for us. My husband was a seminary student—working full-time and going to school full-time—and I was a stay-at-home mother. It was hard work, getting by on what little money we had. There were weeks when renting a movie was a luxury we simply couldn't afford.

As Christmas approached, our son, Samuel, made up his mind about the X-Wing Starfighter model. He had seen it in a local toy store and talked of nothing else for weeks. I had seen it, too, and knew that the price tag of that single toy was more than my entire budget for his Christmas gifts. Plus it was a collector's model, and it was big—the kind of thing you have on display, not the kind of handheld toy that a four-year-old boy runs around the house with, taking out imaginary Death Stars before bedtime.

I had looked around to see if I could get a smaller, cheaper model anywhere, but had come up with nothing. No other store sold anything like it. My heart was broken at the thought of not being able to give my precious child the only thing he asked for. So even though I really didn't understand how big and how awesome our God is, I prayed. How did I think God would answer me? I wasn't sure, but I hoped that somehow, when he opened his little gifts on Christmas morning, Samuel would be happy with what I had bought. Maybe God could fix it so that Samuel would not notice that the X-Wing Starfighter was nowhere to be seen.

Christmas Eve came, and I was in a local store making some last-minute purchases. I was feeling desperate under the weight of this and so many other personal struggles that I was going through back then. As I did every time I visited the store, I walked over to the clearance table to see whether there was anything I could save a few dollars on. To my complete and utter amazement, there on the table was a Star Wars X-Wing Starfighter for less than five dollars! Not only was this toy affordable, it was the perfect size for Samuel's little hands to hold and swoosh around the room.

I stood and stared. First there was a tear, and then the floodgates opened. In the middle of the store, I broke down and cried. In the midst of my desperation, God had found me. I was suddenly aware of just how much He cared about the things that mattered to me; I was overwhelmed with a sense of how much God cared for me. Because of His love I was able to give my child the one gift he had requested.

Jesus tells us in Luke 11 that we should ask, seek, and knock. We should never forget that God loves us, that He cares for us, and that His timing is perfect. And even when we don't know precisely what it is that we need or how we should be asking, God's love and knowledge of us is immense.

Many years have passed since that Christmas, and my four-year-old boy is now in college. But the miracle of that Christmas remains with me—as does the X-Wing Starfighter—reminding me to trust God with every detail of my life and the lives of those I love.

18

A Long Path to Healing

Beverly Underhill

It was sixteen years ago that my sister had a stroke. It was a terrible thing to happen to such a beautiful, vibrant woman. The unexpected, devastating episode left her paralyzed from the neck down. She was only forty-four.

Doctors offered so many different theories about why it happened, or what caused it, but no one knew for sure what was behind it. One thing they were sure of, though, was that Lavana didn't have long to live. After months of rehab and therapy, she was finally able to come home, her husband by her side, honoring the vows he made, "in sickness and in health."

Stripped of all her freedom, completely dependent on others, life became a trial for Lavana. And it got worse. Though she had no control over them, her arms began to contract. It got so horribly painful that five years ago she had to have the muscles cut.

And then just two weeks ago, something miraculous

happened. My sister called me: "I was alone in bed last night," she said. "Everything was quiet, but I felt a hand on my shoulder and heard God tell me, 'Lavana, move your fingers.' I looked down at my hands and began to wiggle my fingers! I know I'm going to be able to move my arms again!"

Between the paralysis and the cut muscles, there were two powerful reasons why she shouldn't be able to move her arms ever again. But if God had spoken, who was I to disagree?

Amazed, grateful, and full of tears, I spent the next few days watching as she began to move her hands and even pull in her arm when her therapist would extend it out. Then to everyone's amazement, she was able to raise herself from a bent position to sitting up.

Her therapists say there's no medical reason why Lavana should be regaining movement like this. But we know that God isn't done with miracles yet. And I have the feeling that He's not yet done with my sister either.

19

Not Unto Death

Margaret Brooks

Growing up in the Bible Belt in a Christian home—with Christian grandparents, aunts, and uncles—was a good thing. Life centered on the church, and I learned the importance of prayer from an early age. By the time I was a teenager, I was ready to give my heart to Jesus. And although I always prayed for others as well as for myself, I never asked anyone to pray for me. I thought that if I was praying for me, why should I tell other people what was going on within me? The truth is I was rather shy. I still am, really. Or I was until four years ago. That's when everything changed.

I had suspected something was wrong for some time, but it was still a shock to sit on that comfortable leather chair in the kind doctor's office and hear the word *cancer*. For some people the moment of diagnosis is the point at which they are overwhelmed by fear. But it didn't work like that for me. Maybe I was numbed by the shock because I began to share my news with my family, friends, and pastors. For the first time in my life, I was hearing people reply with the words, "I'll pray for you."

A week before the bilateral mastectomy, I told the doctors I was worried about a cough that I had been unable to shake for weeks. No one seemed to think it was serious enough to delay the surgery until, the night before the operation, my doctor phoned. "I know you're due to be operated on tomorrow at 8:00 a.m., but I'm not clearing you for surgery, Margaret," she said. I checked my watch: 9:00. It really was the eleventh hour.

Instead of surgery I went in for tests and found that I had acute asthmatic bronchitis. According to the staff, it was so bad that had I gone ahead with the operation, I could have died on the table. My doctor—a wonderful Christian woman—told me that she was going out of town for a seminar but would reschedule the surgery when she got back, giving me time to get over the cough.

The house was quiet when, a few days later, I woke up early and sat with my coffee and my Bible. I was feeling discouraged, knowing that I needed the surgery but unsure of how long I would have to wait. If ever I needed some direction from God, it was then.

I accidentally dropped my Bible and reached to pick it up. As I laid it back on my lap, it fell open, and my eyes immediately landed on John 11:4. The words burned right into me: "This sickness is not unto death, but for the glory of God, that the Son of God might be glorified" (KJV).

"Really?" I prayed. For so long I had been asking God, "Why?" And each time I had felt His reply was, *Why not you?* It had never quite made sense to me, but with this scripture open in front of me, I began to feel overjoyed and started to praise God.

When my doctor returned to work, she called and asked me to see her immediately because she had news for me. I got there that morning, and she greeted me with a big hug. "Something exciting has happened," she said. "While I was at the seminar, I heard about a treatment for your kind of rare cancer. It might reduce the size of the tumor so that surgery won't have to be so invasive."

She told me that the treatment consisted of one tiny pill a day for about nine months, and if I started right away, she would plan on operating later in the year. "I'll see you in thirty days, but don't expect any changes before then. It's going to take five to six months before any noticeable difference can be seen."

I left feeling excited and full of faith. It was now clear why God had kept me out of surgery, and by the time my next month's appointment came around, I knew that something had started to change within me.

My doctor's eyes filled with tears almost straightaway. As she examined me, all she could say was, "Where is it? Where is it? This is a miracle! It's not supposed to happen this way." There was no tumor.

We went along with the protocol for the full nine months and then proceeded to surgery to see whether there were any cancer cells still lurking. There weren't. And even though I had cancer cells in ten out of thirteen lymph nodes—possibly indicating that I had cancer elsewhere in my body—I knew I had been healed and trusted what the Lord had told me.

I decided not to keep anything back from people. I

figured if this cancer was for His glory then I had better be doing my part and spread the word, so I was telling everyone I met about the Lord Jesus. I went through six chemo treatments, and each time, as I sat in the room with the handful of other patients all hooked up to their own IV bags, I told them all about Jesus. I was no longer shy, no longer private; I just wanted to spend every minute of those five-hour treatments telling people what the Lord had done for me.

Some had lost all hope, some were despondent, and some were just lonely and afraid. So many people told me how much they needed to hear my story.

It has now been almost five years since my surgery. All tests show that I am cancer-free. I have been healed by God. I am going to keep on giving Him all the glory and honor, and I also know that even if the cancer comes back tomorrow, it will not take away from the miracle I have already received. If it returns, it will simply mean that God has something else for me to do. And I will praise Him for working in my life.

20

A Prayerful Surrender

Carrie Hass

Thirteen years we had been married. We were nineteen when we fell in love and became man and wife, and in the years that followed we had three wonderful children. But over the past five years, things had started to decline. We were losing contact with each other, becoming disconnected. We could barely get along to save our own lives.

I had attended church consistently, all the time taking my children along with me. And in all the years we had been together, my husband had accompanied us only three times—and then only to support the kids if they were singing or performing.

Not that long ago, things between us had gotten so bad that I had completely checked out emotionally from him. We weren't talking, and the only thing standing in the way of me wanting a divorce was the fact that I didn't want to leave either my kids or my home.

Just about all I could do was pray. As I was getting ready to go to church one Sunday morning, I called out to God with a specific request: "God, if I'm meant to stay in this marriage, then let my husband come to church with me this morning." Like that was ever going to happen.

I heard the front door open and feet climbing the stairs. My husband was back from the gym, and I watched him walk to his closet and start to get ready.

"What are you doing?" I asked.

"I'm going to church," he said. He paused before adding, "But I don't know why."

That day changed my life. Not only was it the day my husband started coming to church, but it was the day I started wearing my wedding band again. God spoke loud and clear to me, telling me that I am to remain in my marriage. Even though there are still struggles, we take them day by day and trust God.

21

Strength for the Tornado

Carolynn Bernard

Where I'm from in Oklahoma, the middle of May is storm season. That's why, on a clear day at the start of summer one year, my neighbor and I decided to clean out the cellar that lay about eighty-five feet from our house. You never know when you're going to need a place to take shelter.

The cellar belonged to us, and it was old, small, and completely underground. Only the door was visible from above ground. Once Margie and I had opened the heavy door—not without a struggle—and crept inside, we found the usual collection of dirt, dust, and spiders, along with a pair of bunk beds.

We carried the four mattresses outside to air out and spent the afternoon cleaning and sweeping until it was ready, should we ever need to use it. Of course, even though the cellar was ours, we invited Margie and her husband to come and use it any time they needed it.

Two or three nights later the storms started to come in. There was a lot of wind, rain, thunder, and lightning. I've always been fearful of storms, so my husband and I were watching the weather on TV, ready to run to the cellar as soon as we needed to.

Sometime around 10:30 p.m., the weatherman said, "There is no severe weather in the state of Oklahoma." I exhaled a little and felt relieved. We put our two children to bed and considered going to sleep ourselves but decided to stay up a little longer.

The wind was still blowing hard, and the thunder and lightning hadn't let up either. Ronnie, my husband, was watching TV, but I was glued to the show taking place outside. I watched as the winds started to change; one minute they were blowing from the north, then from the east, then the south, then the west. I knew this was not normal. "Ronnie," I said, "something's wrong."

More to appease me than because he was worried, Ronnie went to the front door to look out and see if there was anything we should be concerned about. He came back soon enough, saying he didn't see anything to worry about. He knew I was still scared, so he went to look out the back door.

Seconds later he ran back into the living room, yelling, "There's a tornado in the field behind the house! I've got Brady—you get Missy! I'll get the cellar door open. Hurry!" I saw him run out of the front door and head off toward the cellar.

I picked up Missy, our twenty-two-month-old daughter, and followed my husband. I was about sixty-five feet from the cellar when Ronnie had just about reached the door.

That's when I felt as if all the breath was being sucked out of my lungs. In panic I looked around and saw that there was absolutely no wind blowing; even the leaves on the tree were completely still.

I had always heard that in the moment before a tornado strikes everything gets totally still. I was terrified and yelled, "It's got me!"

"Keep running!" Ronnie shouted. But it was dark, and I couldn't see either him or the cellar. Then a flash of lightning lit up the cellar door. Somehow I managed to get there, but Ronnie hadn't gotten the door open yet. He was desperately feeling all over the top of the door but couldn't find the handle. "Forget about the handle," I shouted and reached under the edge of the door. Holding my daughter tightly with one hand, I used the other to throw the heavy door all the way open.

I quickly stepped into the cellar, but in my hurry I missed the first step and rolled the rest of the way down. *Well,* I thought as we tumbled down the stairs, *thank God I'm in the cellar!*

Once I was at the bottom, I checked Missy, and she was okay. I had been wrapped around her while we fell. Amazingly I couldn't feel any immediate damage to myself either. Ronnie was soon down, setting Brady next to me before going back up to shut the door. He tried as hard as he could, but the wind was so strong he couldn't close it. So we huddled together in a corner of the cellar as the tornado passed right over us. "I know who saved us," I said to Ronnie. "And we owe our lives to Him."

Shortly after it passed, our neighbors came running to check on us. We all sat down there in the cellar and talked until we felt it was all over. As we talked, they told me that they had heard the tornado hitting our garage a fraction of a second before they heard me yell to Ronnie. There was no way that it would have taken so long for the tornado to travel from the garage to our cellar. Something—or Someone—must have held the storm back while Missy and I made it to safety.

The next day we started the task of looking over the damage to our property. We found sheet metal in all the trees around the cellar, yet I had never seen any debris flying around while we were desperately working to get in the cellar. Any one of the pieces that we pulled down could have cut us up, and I was so thankful that none of us were hurt or killed.

I had been raised in a Christian home and always went to church, but I had never accepted Jesus as my Lord. Just two weeks after the tornado came through our yard, the Methodist church I was raised in hosted a lay-witness mission, and one of the couples involved was staying at my parents' house. My mom and dad were so touched by their testimony that they called and wanted me to be sure to come with them to church. I went to that meeting, and my life was changed forever.

When the altar call was made, my mom went forward and rededicated her life to the Lord, and God reminded me of what I had said as I fell down the stairs: I owed my life to Him. So, remembering the words I had said to my husband in the shelter, I, too, went to the altar. There I found my hiding place. There I turned all of me over to Jesus.

That was the beginning of the most wonderful relationship I have ever known. I still believe God used that tornado to capture my heart and make me His own, and I believe that it is never too late to turn to Jesus and find His amazing love for you. He knows when, where, and how to reach each one of us. He knew what it would take for me, and I thank Him every day for that tornado.

22

A Soldier and a Car Bomb

Diane Strobeck

My husband had been serving in Afghanistan with the 2nd Battalion, 18th Field Artillery Regiment for about seven weeks. This was his third combat tour, and with three boys at home we tried to have a fifteen- or twenty-minute video call every couple of days.

We were in the middle of one of our video calls one day when my husband broke off the conversation. I watched his eyes flick away from the screen, his body tightening. I could just make out some noises in the background, muffled shouts mainly, but before I could ask what was wrong, he looked back at me and said, "I've gotta go." The last thing I saw was him grabbing his M4 and running out the door.

Nothing like this had ever happened before, and I stayed in front of my computer, not knowing what to do. The screen showed the empty chair where my husband had been sitting, and I strained to hear the background noise and pick up clues about what was going on.

I had a bad feeling. Something told me that I needed to pray. "Lord, watch over my husband and his soldiers. Keep them safe in Your arms. Keep them from harm," I said, before calling family and friends and asking them to pray too.

For two hours I sat in front of the screen, staring at the chair and the door, wondering what was going on beyond them, and praying. I prayed for my husband and the rest of the soldiers, begging God to protect them all from danger.

At about 11:00 p.m., the connection went dead. Somehow I had a feeling that he was okay. But I still stayed up the rest of the night, praying with every minute that passed. And when the boys woke up the next day, I continued with my normal routine, taking care of them, cleaning the house, and trying to stay calm.

It wasn't until that evening that my computer announced I had an incoming call from my husband. It was a sweet relief to see him back in the same chair and hear him say, "There was a situation, but I'm fine." I knew that he couldn't tell me much at the time, but when he said, "There was a situation," I understood enough to know that our prayers had really been important.

Seven months later, when his tour was over and he returned home, I finally heard the full story. A suicide bomber had driven into the front gate, yet for some reason his bomb failed to detonate. The guy was fiddling with the wires, desperate to carry out his mission, when the soldiers managed to pull him out of the car.

According to the translator, the would-be bomber was livid. Even though he had the wires connected, the bomb refused to blow. And when the soldiers eventually did manage to detonate it themselves, it took out the gate and part of the wall, damaging buildings in a quarter-mile area.

Yet not one soldier was hurt.

I know the prayers of my friends and family counted that day, and the words of Psalm 124 resonate louder with me than ever:

> If it had not been the LORD who was on our side . . .
>> when people rose up against us,
> then they would have swallowed us up alive,
>> when their anger was kindled against us . . .
> We have escaped like a bird . . .
> Our help is in the name of the LORD,
>> who made heaven and earth. (ESV)

23

Divine Appointment

M. A. Pasquale

I began the day as I did any other, waking to an early alarm clock, saying prayers of thanks to God, making lunches for my husband and kids, and driving into work while listening to K-LOVE and worshiping all the way. When you're caring for sick and hurting hospital patients, you learn to rely on God. "What would You have me do today?" I prayed.

I was a contract occupational therapy assistant, and over the years God had provided me with many wonderful opportunities, not just to pray with and comfort other believers but also to plant seeds with those who weren't saved yet. As soon as I arrived at work that morning, I grabbed my list of people to see, reviewed their charts, and hit the ground running.

Halfway through my day I read the chart of my next patient—a middle-aged man I will call John. I asked his nurse if I could work with him. When I spoke with her, she became visibly upset, tears gliding down her cheeks. She had obviously been his nurse for some time and had great compassion for him. She told me how the doctors had her call his wife to come in from work to discuss his prognosis—which was as bad as it gets. His bodily systems were failing, and they expected him to die soon. There was nothing more they could do for him.

When patients reach this point—when they're dying or going to hospice—occupational therapists will discharge them. That's just the way it's done. But I knew God was urging me to go into his room and speak with him. So I asked the nurse if I could see him anyway just to talk.

When I entered John's room, I found a tall, swollen man stumbling to the bed from the bathroom. He appeared completely worn-out with nothing to say as all this bad news was sinking in. He sat on the bed, and as I introduced myself, his wife walked in. From the look on her face, it was clear that she was expecting the worst.

Ask them if they know Me. I knew God was speaking to me, and I blurted out, "Do you know Jesus Christ as your Lord and Savior?"

They both silently shook their heads no.

"Would you like to pray with me now to receive Christ?"

They both nodded yes. It was all happening so fast that it was hard to take in, yet I knew that this was what God wanted me to do. As we bowed our heads and held hands, I led them in prayer, asking for healing, and we prayed the sinner's prayer. We finished as a doctor was entering the room, and I thanked them, said good-bye, and found a bathroom where I could cry.

I was amazed and grateful to God for the opportunity to see a man and his wife surrender their lives to God, but the story doesn't end there. A month or so later I was back at that same hospital and ran into John's nurse, the one who had cried for him that day. As I asked her about him, her eyes grew large, and a smile spread over her face.

"He didn't die after all. Somehow he got better and was discharged!" she said.

Somehow he got better? I knew there was no mystery to it at all. God had touched him and healed him both physically and spiritually. What an awesome blessing to be a part of the amazing things He does.

And one day, I know, I'll get to hear the rest of John's story.

24

Falling Toward God

Tammy Siligrini

He heals the brokenhearted and binds up their wounds.

Psalm 147:3 niv

I know these words from the psalmist are true. How? My heart once was broken and my soul wounded. I experienced pain that was worse than any I could have ever imagined—worse than any I had feared—and yet here I am, free to forgive. My heart is still beating even though the scars remain.

It was the early morning of September 29, 2012, when I heard my phone ringing. I looked at the phone's display; it was the mother of my son's fiancée. Why would she be calling me this early? Could it have something to do with James? James was the most forgiving and loving person I knew, with a smile that would light up a room and the kind of personality that could change any negative situation. He touched many people in the community and was loved. And he was a new father to his three-month-old son, Aiden. Could that be why she was calling?

But it wasn't about Aiden. It was James. She told me that there had been a terrible accident and that my precious nineteen-year-old son was gone. I screamed so loud that I woke my sister up from a deep sleep. She came rushing into the room where I was staying, thinking I was having a bad dream. The reality was so much worse than any nightmare.

As I explained what little I knew to her, I realized that I had hung up the phone without asking any questions. I had no idea where they had taken my son. Where was he? Where was my boy? I called back, found out the name of the hospital, and then called my husband to come pick up my sister and me on the way there.

It felt unreal. Standing outside the hospital at 5:30 a.m. with my husband and sister, I hesitated. If I went inside, then it all would be real. If I stayed out there in the cold, would it all go away? Would my boy come back to life?

I walked in, through doors that opened without me touching them, pulling me in toward James. Gianna—James's fiancée—was there, crying, hugging me, repeating the words, "I'm sorry, I'm sorry." It was real. This was happening.

A nurse told us where to go. And then I was there— standing in the doorway, staring at the bed where James was lying. He was perfectly still. He looked as though he was sleeping, but his chest was stone. I kissed his head and felt the coldness of his skin on my lips. This would be my last kiss. There would be no more. Before I could hold him, the room filled up with nurses, rushing in to tell me that I could not touch my son. They told me that because he was only nineteen years old and had died at home, there would have to be an autopsy.

I collapsed to the floor, devastated. In my mind questions were piling up on each other. *What happened to him? Was there a chance he knew what was going on as his heart beat out its last? Did he suffer at all, or was it over instantly?* So many questions were weighing me down that I simply couldn't stand.

I was helped up and into a quiet room, where Gianna explained to me what had happened. The night before, James had met up with a friend of his who had a large prescription of narcotic painkillers with him. They were both popping pills, and when James went to bed, he never woke up. That was it.

I called my pastor and told him what had happened. He said he was on his way to the hospital. And then I called Dawn, my best friend—and the woman James had chosen to call Mom. Things had not always been easy between James and me, and his drug use was what we argued about so much. When I told him he could no longer live with me because he was using, it was Dawn who took him into her house. She gave him just one rule while he lived with her, and that was that he had to go to church with her on Sundays. I couldn't get James to go to church, but Dawn did. In the time that he spent with her, James had given his life over to Jesus. But he still struggled with his addiction.

As I sat with others outside the hospital, grieving, waiting for the pastor to get to the hospital, a woman I had never seen before came to the doorway. She came up to the group of us and told us that she felt the Holy Spirit was leading her to pray for us. So she prayed, and as she did, she asked God to bring us together in spite of all the strife that troubled our family. She knew nothing about us, not even why we were in the hospital.

Later that day my husband and I went to Dawn's, where she and I cried on her front porch, calling out for Jesus. We both knew that if we were going to get through this, it would be only by the power and love of Jesus Christ. Without that, we were finished.

Over the next few days there were more tasks to complete and a funeral to plan. We sat in the funeral home, making decisions about flowers and songs and what kind of coffin James would have. And all the time I was wondering how we were going to pay for it all. I prayed, asking God to provide, and friends helped set up donation jars throughout our town. If we were going to get the money, God would have to step in; we knew that if we didn't raise five thousand dollars, the funeral wouldn't happen.

So I prayed even more. We all did. I trusted God to come through on this. And He did, right at the last minute. The night before the funeral we finally had enough money to cremate my son. The funeral director said he had never seen a cash funeral paid off in such a short amount of time, and I knew that we were truly blessed by God's own hand. He even provided food and a place to gather after the funeral, giving us more than we needed, more than we had asked of Him.

But God provided more than just money and food and a place to meet. He provided me with strength. If not for Him, I still would be collapsed on the hospital room floor, unable to get to my feet. But He was with me, guiding me, filling me with everything I needed, especially when, after the funeral,

I was in contact with the friend with whom James was doing the drugs. I just had a feeling I needed to reach out to this young man, and as we talked, I realized this kid was truly sorry for what had happened. Over and over again he told me it should have been him who had died, but I knew differently.

I told him that it was not his time. I told him that God loves him and He has a plan for him. The Spirit led me to publicly forgive him, even though I knew my words would hurt some of the people I loved. But I did it; I forgave him, and it set me free.

God really does heal the brokenhearted and bind up their wounds. And as He does it, He draws others closer to Him. The woman in the hospital, the boy who shared the drugs with James, my friend Dawn who wept with me—all of us broken, all of us invited in by God.

25

A Gift of Life

Robin Williams

Our Mommy & Me class was at a park. I was sitting with the infant group while Kimmie, my toddler, was off with the toddler group. Something pulled me out of the conversation I was in. It was a voice, male, asking, "Where's Kimmie?"

When I looked up, I couldn't see who might have asked such a question. The only people around me were other moms and their babies. I looked back down at the baby in my arms, but again I heard the voice. The question was the same, but this time it was more urgent; this time I couldn't ignore it. I wondered why no one else heard it, and as my eyes scanned the scene, I noticed a pond nearby. I knew I had to get there.

I ran to the water. Even before I had reached it, I could see her, my Kimmie, floating on the surface about fifteen feet away from the side. I waded in and pulled her up out of the water. Right then, in that moment, I was fairly certain she was dead. I screamed for help as I headed back to the side.

One of the moms in the group had just taken a CPR class, and she took over. I watched as she got to work on Kimmie. By the time the paramedics arrived, my beautiful toddler was screaming. It was an amazing sound.

I don't know whether it was God's voice I heard or an angel's, but I praise and thank God every day for what He did thirty-two years ago. I was shown God's mercy, and I learned a valuable lesson: never, ever ignore His command. Ever since that day, whenever God tells me to move, I move.

26

God's Plan Is Good

Pat Stone

The engine was steaming. Through the dirt that half-covered the windshield, I could see that I was now facing the wrong way down the road. I needed to get help. I powered down the window, turned the key, and prayed, "Lord, send me help. It'll be getting cold soon."

It was December 3, 2003, and for once I didn't have a car full of kids. I had been on my way to serve on a grand jury, careful of the conditions on the roads as the recent warmer weather would have melted much of the snow. As I had headed round the corner, I hit ice, felt the car lurch from my control, and braced myself for the inevitable impact.

My head hurt. I reached up and felt a large bump on the top of my head. I leaned forward to look out my open window. Immediately a sharp pain shot through my neck. I carefully leaned back in the seat. To my amazement, I heard a car coming from behind me. I stuck out my hand and waved for help, glad that God had sent me help so fast.

At the hospital the doctor confirmed the worst: I had broken my neck. What was worse was the fact that both the front and back of the same vertebra were broken, with the risk of the spinal cord within being damaged. It was a serious injury, the sort that could easily leave me paralyzed.

But somehow I didn't see it that way. All I could think was that God had intervened so far—and not just with the accident. Some years earlier I had been treated for thyroid cancer, and God had gotten me through that one. As far as I could tell, the doctor just needed to do his job and God would take care of the results.

After a while I was told that I was lucky. The break had been serious, but my spinal cord was fine. I told them about the treatment for the thyroid cancer and how I had had a bone scan to monitor the level of bone strength after treatment. I explained to the doctors that I had excellent bone density. Had I not, then perhaps the spinal cord would have been damaged, and I would have been paralyzed below the neck.

But as much as I knew that God was at work back then, my sense of Him being in control grew stronger and stronger with time. And when August 2005 came around and our youngest son, Matthew, fell ill, I knew why I had been saved from being paralyzed. We had always called Matthew our bonus baby because he has an extra chromosome and, therefore, Down syndrome. He was only ten in the summer of 2005 when he was diagnosed with acute lymphocytic leukemia. For the next three and a half years, the family all cared for Matthew, and I had a renewed joy in knowing that God's sovereign plan for me is perfect.

Even as I lay in the hospital back in 2003 with my neck brace on, I knew that I could trust God. I knew that He knows the plans He has for my life, and being paralyzed was not a part of them. Why did God take me through this? The explanation is simple: I am God's vessel, and He will shape my life as He sees fit.

27

Light at the End of the Tunnel

Justin King

Sometimes you can't see the light at the end of the tunnel. Sometimes things are so dark and the air is so close that you can't even see the tunnel. That was me, and I didn't think I would ever get out. But then, at just the right time, God sent me an angel who happened to look a lot like my mom.

I was twenty-one years old when my body started failing me. For a week I experienced back pain so severe that it left me lying on the floor in tears. By week two I was growing weaker and was unable to walk unaided into the ER. Bit by bit I watched my body stop working.

The doctors told me I had Guillain-Barré syndrome, a rare nerve disorder that attacks the sheath around the nervous system and prevents the brain from sending signals to the rest of the body. It's like your body's Internet goes down, leaving your brain more and more isolated. Sometimes the paralysis that Guillain-Barré syndrome inflicts is permanent; sometimes it is fatal.

I was admitted to the hospital, sent to the ICU, and placed on a ventilator. For eight days I thought I was living my final hours. Everyone else did too . . . my family, my doctors. They all thought that death was only moments away. My parents sat by my bed, watching me sign "I love you" to them until the pain grew to be too much and the tears ran down my face.

I didn't know much about God before I got sick, and I didn't get to know Him at all during my sickness. But I thought about Him often. I wondered how the God who was supposed to be so kind and loving could do something like this to someone. I wondered if He was laughing at me as my body slowly shut down. Maybe He didn't care. Maybe He wasn't even there anyway.

I was at the age when I was supposed to be full of energy and optimism, but instead, just as my body had shut down, my spirit fell into a state of depression. Like my increasingly isolated brain, I was cut off from my friends and family.

The day I came off the ventilator was the day I reached my breaking point. I told my family that I had had enough. I told them that I was done trying and just wanted to die.

"I quit."

"I know you do," my mother said. "But there's a light at the end of the tunnel, Justin. You just need to have faith that you'll see it one day."

Slowly I began to get a little better. Plasmapheresis recycled my blood and removed the bad antibodies, but the journey out of that state of physical weakness and emotional depression was long and hard. I was forced to wear diapers, and the shame of it made me feel worse. Even though my body was getting better, my soul was getting worse. Eight months after my diagnosis I was able to leave the hospital and return home in a wheelchair. I had gone from 170 pounds of muscle to a 100-pound shadow of a man who looked like a cartoon character of skin and bones. I turned twenty-two in that chair, and I was determined not to be in it when I turned twenty-three.

I wish I could say that this was where my trials ended and the tunnel's ending came into view. I would love to be able to say that this was the point where I grabbed hold of God and refused to let go. But it wouldn't be true. Instead, I was one of those hardheaded kids whose life turns around at the speed of a glacier.

My body might have improved enough to get me discharged from the hospital, but my head was in no better shape than it had been the day I told my mom that I wanted to end it all. I was still depressed, and I had been isolated for so long that I didn't know at all how to share my dark feelings with my family or friends. On my own I couldn't make sense of what was going on inside me, and I needed a way out. I chose drugs. For the next couple of months, I spent every dollar I had saved and every moment I was awake using cocaine. I needed something to stop me from sleeping all the time, and I felt when I was high I could remember just a little of how I used to feel back in the days before all this happened.

I have lost count of the number of times I took too much and risked blowing my heart out. I guess I didn't care whether the numbness was temporary or permanent, whether I lived or died. I felt myself slowly giving in to the tunnel's darkness. But God had a different plan for my life.

I was sitting in my room one day, curtains closed, getting high, when my mom opened the door and came in. She didn't scream. She didn't tell me to stop or pretend it hadn't happened. She just spoke, quietly and calmly:

"I'm so disappointed in you, Justin."

And then she walked out. My heart, which I had tried for so long to numb into oblivion, suddenly ached with the pain of brokenness. I knew in that very moment that I needed to change. If not, I would die.

The choice between death and rehab wasn't hard. I joined a facility that helped me find my way forward again. And even though I stumbled at first, I gradually began to see that in those dark months of hospital beds and darkened bedrooms, I hadn't been alone after all. God had been with me the whole time, whether I knew it or not.

Eight days later it was time to return home. I was still using a cane to walk and had no feeling at all in my feet because of the nerve damage, but I felt as though, finally, I was alive again. As I drove the sixty miles back home to Loris, South Carolina, about the only thing I could do was cry. My eyes were finally open, and I could see all the many blessings I had around me: a loving family and friends, safety, hope, and the love and forgiveness of God Himself. As I was driving toward the house, the local K-LOVE station began playing a song that made my tears flow even faster. The lyrics spoke of the confusion that often accompanies suffering, but there was one line that stood out over all the others:

There's a light at the end of this tunnel.

If ever there was a sign that God was with me, that was it. It was all I needed, and the timing was perfect.

In time I started participating regularly in church, and these days I have found a new way to cope with life: trusting in my Savior. I'm still clean, and I do my best to give God the glory in all my accomplishments and give Him the glory when I get through any hardships. And I know this one thing to be true: while God can be found in the light at the tunnel's end, He is also there in the darkness with you. Always.

28

God's Whisper

Teresa Lindsay

It's 10:00 p.m., and I'm just about done on this warm Texas summer's night. I'm about to put Brooklyn, my one-year-old daughter, to bed, and pretty soon after that I'll be asleep myself. But the phone rings.

It's work. Darrel has lost his keys and can't lock up the gym. Can I do it? Sure. I'll be right over. I don't mind doing it. It's a nice night for a drive.

I pick up my sleepy daughter and place her in her car seat, right behind the driver's seat. With the windows rolled down we make our way out into the night. There's not much traffic around as I drive through the residential neighborhood, down roads with two lanes on either side. Just as we reach the top of a small hill, I have the strangest impression that I need to slow down and move over into the right-hand lane. Seems like a crazy idea to me, and between the darkness and all the cars parked over there on the right, I decide to dismiss the thought out of hand.

But it comes back. *Slow down. Veer to the right.* The thought is insistent and clear, and I decide to do exactly what I am being told. I drop to twenty miles per hour and pull over to the right so that I am not in the path of any oncoming traffic.

Right away I see a car coming toward me, heading straight at me from a side road on the left. He is not stopping and is going to T-bone me, smashing right into both my daughter and me. I pull hard on the steering wheel, sending us up over the curb and onto the sidewalk, away from the oncoming car. I am shaking uncontrollably and crying. I check behind me; Brooklyn has slept through it all.

I breathe deep and get my composure back. I look back down the road I've come along. I can still see the driver, still swerving from side to side as though he has never driven before. I guess he is drunk, and it hits me that though the danger has passed for me, there is still a risk of him crashing into someone else. I decide to turn around, follow him, and flash my high beams to everyone he is approaching. I do exactly that, and the moment a car comes toward us I start flashing. The first car flashes back, too, only his lights are blue and red. He pulls the crazy driver over, and I go on my way, thanking God that even though I was stubborn and refused to listen to His first warning, He gave me a second chance to experience His loving protection.

29

Joy Out of Pain

Rebecca Backen

June 6, 1973, was a big day in our house. It marked the moment that Mom, after many years of being a housewife, finally finished her probationary period in her new job. "After midnight," she told us, "you can get sick from anything you want; for the first time in our lives we'll have health coverage."

School had just gotten out for the summer, and my dad was going on an overnight haul to Fresno, California. I was twelve years old and loved nothing more than to go on those long hauls with Dad, so I begged to be allowed to accompany him. My parents said yes, and I had a wonderful time sitting next to him while he drove. The last thing I remember is watching the sun rise in Fresno on June 7, and seeing the women's prison there. After that it's all a blank, until I woke up in the hospital.

What I found out later was that in the afternoon, just as we were nearing home, we stopped at a small grocery store in

Helendale. It was hot, and Dad said I could go swimming in a nearby reservoir, but as we were preparing to drive over the railroad tracks, something happened—we stalled.

Suddenly there was a train coming down the track. Even though it had slowed to sixty miles per hour, it hit my side of the semi with enough force to throw me out of the passenger door and barrel the truck down the track.

It took almost twenty-five minutes for the ambulance to arrive, and even though they found my dad right away, they had to search for me. They eventually found me, lying in a ditch about fifty yards from the road. I had landed face-first and slid several feet, and it was clear that I was in real trouble. I was taken to the hospital and found to have broken my nose and my cheekbones, detached my right eye, broken a couple of ribs, and had a collapsed lung. My right pelvic bone was broken and had been shoved into my abdomen. My right thigh bone was also broken and my right ankle crushed. The area below my right knee and extending to the top of the foot had been shredded, with most of the shinbone and all of the muscle scooped away. I had lost a lot of blood, and the fact that my AB positive blood type is not common only added yet another complication to the long list of problems the doctors were facing.

My mom was at the hospital, listening as a team of doctors told her the extent of my injuries. One repeated that they did not expect me to survive while another told her that if I did, the severity of my brain trauma meant that I would certainly be spending whatever life I had left in a vegetative state. "Your daughter's heart has already stopped beating once," he said, "and we're having great difficulty stabilizing her."

From outside my room my mother could hear me moaning and doctors and nurses talking about what they were going to do. She heard them discuss scrubbing out the leg with a wire brush, and then she heard them yell that my heart had stopped again. One of the doctors came back out and told her that they were going to have to open my skull since I was not responding to anything or anyone and they were afraid bone chips had penetrated my brain.

Mom was allowed in to see me, though she didn't recognize me. She said my head was so swollen that it looked like a basketball with a mouth. She bent over and told me that she loved me. Amazingly I told her that I loved her too. It was the first response anyone had gotten from me. The doctors decided not to open my head.

Though I remember nothing of the accident, I do recall one moment from my time in the emergency room. I remember standing up and watching doctors and nurses work over someone on a stretcher. There was a flash of light, and I turned to see what it was. A door was glowing, and I walked toward it. When I stretched out my hand to turn the knob, the door opened, and the most beautiful man I've ever seen walked in.

"Becky," he said, "I'm here for you. God sent me to tell you that it is very important for you to stay here. He has a plan for you, and this is part of it."

I asked him who he was. He laughed and said his name was Joseph.

"Am I the person on the bed, Joseph?"

"Yes."

"Is this going to hurt?"

"Yes," he said. "But every time it gets too bad for you, I will come and take you out of it for a breather."

I must have gone back to my room because the next thing I knew, Joseph was standing beside me while I was lying on a bed. He held his hand out and said, "Becky, come talk to me."

I got up, and we went to the other side of the room. Joseph reminded me that God loves me very much and that all of this was His plan. I asked how my dad was, and he told me that he would be fine. We talked about Mom and my sister, Sally. I felt very safe and secure, kind of warm. Then he said, "Back you go."

We spoke three times, and for years I thought it had all been a dream. When I found out that my heart had stopped three times while I was in the ER, I started to wonder whether it might have been something more than a hallucination.

After six hours of surgery the doctors decided that since we had Kaiser insurance, I had to be transported to the Kaiser hospital in Fontana, California. Mom was told that I probably wouldn't survive the trip, but they couldn't keep me there.

I made it to Kaiser and was bandaged, sewn up in places, and put in traction. They rolled me off to a cubicle and said to my mom, "Well, it's up to her now. There's nothing else we can do."

I don't know if it was the next day or the next week, but I eventually woke up. I recognized people, and while I couldn't speak due to a trachea tube, I could communicate by writing. Eventually the tube was taken out, and I was moved to the pediatrics wing. My nose and cheekbones straightened themselves out without any doctor ever having to reset anything, and my right eye reattached itself.

Doctors couldn't decide what to do about my leg. Some wanted to amputate while one fought for keeping it. My pelvic bone was put back into place, my thigh bone reset, and after a month in pediatrics, I was taken to surgery for skin grafting and put in a body cast. On August 3, two months after the accident, I was sent home.

My dad was also at home, as he needed Mom's help with his recovery, but gradually we both got better. In December I was back at Kaiser for a week, to learn how to walk on crutches, and by the end of January 1974, I was tired of the crutches, so I decided it was time to walk . . . and I did. Even though I had been told that I would never walk again, within a year I could ride a bike and walk long distances.

There was one thing that did look like it would be impossible to overcome: my doctor said that due to the accident, I could not have children. The damage done by the pelvic bone could not be undone. I was brokenhearted about that and had tests done repeatedly. Not only was I sterile, but there were bone spurs on the pelvic bone that would tear up my uterus if I ever did manage to become pregnant.

Imagine my surprise when, two years into my marriage, I found out I was pregnant. I was immediately given an ultrasound, which revealed that there were no bone spurs around my uterus. On April 10, 1989, I gave birth to a beautiful, healthy, full-term girl. She was followed in 1991 by a wonderful boy. And, as a further surprise, they were followed in 2003 by another little girl.

My life is full of miracles, and I am grateful for what happened. I became a more caring person and have been made stronger by the knowledge that God has been with me all the way. I thank Him for this life, both the pain and the joy.

30

They Met My Need

Yvonne Podruchny

In some ways we had been through it all before. Just one year earlier my sister had been forced to withdraw from school before beginning her senior year. My grandmother's bookstore was struggling, and she didn't have the money to pay the fees. It looked as though I would have to drop out at some point, too, but a teacher and his wife had stepped in and offered to pay the whole lot.

This year, although my sister had graduated, we were facing the same financial difficulties. The kind teacher and his wife had decided to pay for their niece and nephew's tuitions in another state, which left us grateful for their previous support but desperate to see God in action.

There was a reason why it mattered so much to me. I had been raised in a Christian home and was in love with Jesus; I didn't want to go anywhere but the Christian school I had been attending since first grade.

So once again my grandma and I turned to God. She filled out the enrollment papers, and as we sat in the car outside the school, she asked me to take them in. I didn't want to do it on my own, so after pleading with her for a little while, we both went into the office together.

"Well," said the treasurer as soon as we walked in, "do you want to hear good news or great news?" She went on to tell us that an older couple, whom we didn't know, had just left the office saying they wanted to do something good for someone. "I told them about you, and they agreed to pay all your tuition. All you have to do in return is pray for them."

I was so excited and humbled by their generosity, and I happily accepted both their gift and my prayer assignment.

And when the start of my senior year came around and the older couple was unable to keep paying, I knew to trust God for my final year fees. And sure enough, my uncle and aunt said that they wanted to pay, and I graduated just as I always hoped I would—from my Christian school and with my faith stronger than ever.

31

Journey

Jan Gibson

I need to be clear right from the start. I am not the kind of person who goes on mission trips. I have none of the special skills that seem to be required, and my husband has always been just as against the idea as I have. And I've never had any kind of desire to go to Africa. At least, that's how I used to be. Then 2006 happened, and God spoke about as clearly as He has ever spoken to me about anything. He told me to go. And when He says go, it's a good idea to be obedient.

It all started when my friend Patty and I volunteered in our church's children's department. As we waited for the children to come in one Sunday morning, I listened to several people discussing an upcoming mission trip to Mozambique; the plan was to travel out there and teach volunteers how to do vacation Bible school. There was an information meeting that afternoon for anyone who wanted to know more.

Now, Patty has always been energetic and enthusiastic,

and she turned to me and said, "We should go along too." To humor her, I agreed, but I knew that an information meeting was about as close as I was ever going to get to a mission trip to Mozambique. Yet something must have happened at the meeting because in the days that followed I felt as though my heart was being tugged toward Africa. Every time I turned around it was as if I saw something that had to do with Africa: I walked into a classroom for a meeting, and there was a huge map of Africa on the wall; I opened my state's gardening magazine to a two-page spread of Africa; I turned on the TV, and there was Africa. Something strange was going on.

I decided to pray about it, and over the following weeks I could tell that something inside me was shifting. I gradually softened to the idea, but it wasn't until the night I got on my knees and refused to move until God made it clear what He wanted me to do, that I finally knew—I was going.

After that came a whole string of obstacles, overcome by God alone. I needed shots, a physical, and twenty-five hundred dollars. I'm really not comfortable asking people for money, but I sent out letters to the people I felt God wanted me to ask for prayer and monetary support. And people sent money!

Just before the deadline, I knew that I was still more than four hundred dollars short, but I asked the missions pastor how much I still owed. "You're good to go," he said. Now, I knew that wasn't true because I hadn't given him any more money, so I asked him to double-check. When he did, he showed me a deposit that I did not make, or know about, for the exact amount I owed.

"Where did that come from?" I asked.

"I don't know," he said. "Someone just gave it."

I found out that some of the shots I needed were covered by my insurance, and some of them I was eligible for through my job. Because I had been diagnosed with ulcerative colitis many years earlier, my new doctor insisted I have a colonoscopy. After the procedure my old specialist came to me and said, "Who told you that you had ulcerative colitis?"

"You did," I said.

"Well," he said, "there's no sign of it anywhere now."

And there were other things that happened, like my father falling ill a couple of months before I was due to depart for the trip. For a while I thought it would put an end to my African plans. But Dad got better in good time.

Then there was the problem with the plane tickets. They had been booked using my nickname, instead of the name on my passport, and it was going to cost an additional four hundred dollars to change it so that I could actually travel. There was no way I could afford that, so I took a friend's advice and went to the airport one day to see if I could talk to someone. Within a matter of minutes I was walking back out with my name changed on my tickets at no charge at all.

As the day of my departure approached, I still didn't know why God wanted me in Africa, but I knew beyond all doubt that He wanted me to go. And it didn't take long into the trip before I found out that He had chosen each of us for our particular talents and that He had each of us exactly where He wanted us. I will never forget my time in Africa and will be forever amazed at the way He works and takes care of each detail.

And by the way, I really, really want to go back.

32

Stuck

Jackie Philp

I was waiting for a certain phone call from my seventy-one-year-old stepmom, whom we all called Nana. She was going to tell me about the result of her PET scan, and I hoped to God that she was going to be able to tell me that it showed no sign of lung cancer. The thought of losing Nana terrified me. If she died, I didn't know what I was going to do.

Nana was a godsend who entered my life when I was sixteen and made me a strong, confident young woman. She was the one who believed in me even when I was quite a teenage handful. She saw the true worth of everyone and loved just as God loved. Nana was my support, my companion in prayer, my compass that sent me back to God.

As I grew up, I learned to love her even more. I loved how, when she joined us to watch my son competing in a spelling bee, she would be so caught up in the experience that her blood pressure would go sky-high and her heart would pound at a hundred miles an hour. I swear she almost passed out when he made it to the regionals.

Nana's call came one evening. I was cleaning the kitchen after dinner. She started speaking the way she always did—a little high on nervous energy, full of extremes and big statements. She spoke like she lived—full of love and excitement.

"What an awful day I had, Jackie. I got confused and went to the wrong hospital for my scan, so I didn't get it. And then my day fell apart."

"What happened?" I replied.

"Well, when I missed the appointment, I figured I could take a quick look at the new Tony's market. I walked in and reached for the Sani-Wipe dispenser to clean the cart, and my thumb got stuck in the dispenser. It was brand-new, and I couldn't get my thumb out."

"Really? That's kinda funny." I was trying not to laugh too much.

"No, it's not!" Nana replied, giggling herself. "I was stuck, and my hand hurt. I had to wait for another customer to come in. What with it being so early in the morning, I had to wait awhile."

"So then what?"

"Well, the lady couldn't get my thumb out either, so she got the manager. He couldn't manage to get my thumb out either and wanted to call the fire department."

"Really? The fire department? Oh, Nana!" I couldn't help laughing at this point, but I recovered quickly enough to ask whether she was okay now and whether the fire department did come.

"No, Jackie, I was not about to have the fire department

come to get my thumb out of a Sani-Wipe dispenser. The manager decided to get the pharmacist, to see if there was something he could do first. Well, between the lady who got the manager, the manager, the pharmacist, and a tub of Vaseline, my thumb finally came out!"

"Thank goodness! Kinda funny looking back, huh?"

"No . . . my hand was purple, and I wanted to leave, but the pharmacist insisted I stay ten minutes! He wanted to know that the color would come back and my hand was okay. I really wanted to just get home."

"Well, I am sure he was just concerned. But it's not that bad."

"Wait, Jackie, it doesn't end there. When I did get home, your father was waiting for me to go out to RadioShack right away because his diabetic meter was out of batteries. I had to go right back out, and as I pulled into RadioShack, the shopping center was full of police cars. The lights weren't on, so I parked and walked to the store. A police officer opened the door, and he told me that RadioShack was robbed and the clerk had been shot ten minutes ago!"

"What? Oh my! Are you kidding me, Nana?"

"No, I am not kidding you, Jackie. What a horrible day, huh?"

I didn't have to think about my response. I was sure that she was wrong about the day being horrible. In my mind she had just been on the receiving end of a wonderful, God-given miracle.

"No, Nana," I said. "This was the best day of your life. God literally held your hand, stopped you, and kept you where He could protect you for those ten minutes. What would have happened if you had turned up in the middle of that robbery?"

"Oh, Jackie, I didn't think about it that way."

And that was it. I guess we all struggle from time to time to see things the right way. Sometimes we're just too close to the situation to see what God is doing. But I learned then—and I'm still learning today—that sometimes, even when life looks like it's all going wrong, God is never far away. And maybe He might just be holding your hand. Literally!

33

My Miracle

Sandra Huffman

I was on a roll at Bible study last Wednesday. I was talking about how even though it can be so hard at times to pay the bills and have enough money for gas or food, God always finds a way. Always. And then this week, back at Bible study, God made it clear to me just how right I was.

We were just about to finish our evening together when one of the ladies came up to me and placed twenty dollars in my hand. "God told me to give this to you at Bible study last week," she said, "but I told Him I had no money to give. Then on Monday, as I was driving by your house to take my kids to school, God told me again: *Give her the twenty dollars.* But again I told Him that I didn't have any money. Finally, just as I drove into the school drop-off circle, a twenty-dollar bill got caught by the wind and blew right up to my car door. *Here's the money,* said God. So here I am, giving it to you."

I was amazed. In my hands was enough money for gas for the rest of the workweek.

I am so thankful to God, not just for bringing the right amount of money along to me at the right time but for the way He chooses us to be a part of the plan. He could have blown twenty dollars on my own car door, yet instead He chose to draw one of His children into the adventure.

God doesn't just meet the needs we're talking about at Bible study—the ones that cause us to worry, like money— but He also meets our deeper needs, such as being a part of His plan to show the world He loves them. All you and I have to do is be available and obedient. If we do that, then who knows in what kind of miracles God will choose to involve us.

34

A Son Restored

Janeen Slider

As a Christian parent, I tried to raise my son to follow Jesus, but that old adage is true—"you can lead a horse to water, but you can't make him drink." Steven had chosen a different path and, because of a conflict between the two of us, cut off all communication with me. A move out of state resulted in not seeing or talking with him for over fifteen months. And because of where we left things, I just had to see him. While traveling back to Virginia for another son's graduation from Liberty University, I shared my hopes with my sister of finding and reconnecting with Steven.

After Jonathan's graduation, when all the photos had been taken and the celebration completed, we said good-bye. It was now time for my sister and me to continue our trip and find my other son.

The traffic was very heavy from the graduation, and the drive was slow, but we enjoyed conversation as sisters do. As we drove toward Norfolk, I saw a familiar-looking truck, one that looked like Steven's white Ford F-150, with a beat-up toolbox in the back. We were both turning off the highway, and the truck ahead was turning left in the same direction I was going.

"That truck looks like Steven's," I said. We both looked closer, and as we did, I thought the driver looked a lot like him as well. My sister agreed, so we followed the truck. I don't know what I was thinking; it all seemed a little wild, but I kept on looking and looking and hoping and hoping. Could this be the way that God was answering my prayers? The truck turned a corner, and that was when I knew—it was Steven.

God had timed the heavy traffic to place me exactly where I needed to be to find my son. The direction in which I was supposed to go would have taken me on a different path, but I was determined to follow the old white truck. After about two miles the truck made a right turn, just up ahead of me. I turned right at the street before, and my sister asked me why I hadn't followed behind the truck. I just felt that turning where we did was the right way to go. After making the turn, I looked to my left and could see the truck going up the street parallel to us. I then turned left on the second street we came to and went to the end of the street. And there he was, my Steven. We pulled in front of his truck to stop it from moving. I jumped out of the car and was by Steve's door as he got out. I hung my arms around his neck and wept.

"Mom," said my son, "you really creeped me out! I was looking in my rearview mirror, wondering why this little red car was following me. Then it dawned on me, it might be you. How have you been?"

And that was it. We were back.

God reunited me with my son, and now we are talking again. Now I have him back in my life. There is work to be done—hard work, I know—but I am grateful to Jesus for the chance to rebuild my relationship with my son. I am so grateful for second chances.

35

Saving Chris

Diane Marino

"Check on Chris!"

I stirred in my bed. The voice sounded urgent, but I was tired and deep in my sleep. With a newborn son in the crib, sleep mattered more than ever.

"Check on Chris!"

Again the voice called to me. This time I came far enough out of my sleep to recognize that something needed to be done. So I nudged my husband. He rolled over and went back to sleep. I chose to ignore the voice and let myself drift again.

Suddenly the room filled with light. I was immediately awake, my eyes drawn to the source at the foot of the bed. Amazed, I saw a large figure standing there. "Check on Chris!"

I ran to the crib. All I could see was his lightweight blanket. I frantically pulled at it and watched in horror as my son's tiny body flipped multiple times out from the cloth. He landed on the mattress, gulping in the life-giving air that he had been starved of in the tangled blanket. I held him close.

God had sent an angel to save my son.

36

Your Will Above All

Kimberly Rivers

In the dream, I was holding her—a beautiful baby girl. Someone approached me, and I let her take a peek. "Oh," she said, sounding disappointed. "It's *another* girl."

"Yes," I said. "This is Adalyn Faith."

"Why did you choose the middle name Faith?" she asked.

"Because I have faith that God knows what He is doing."

The dream ended, I woke up, and I knew then that the baby who had been growing inside me for the past six weeks— my fourth child—would be called Adalyn Faith. But I had no idea how relevant that name would be.

Shortly after Adalyn's first birthday, she became very fussy. She was in pain the majority of the time, and over a two-week period I took her to the doctor seven times, seeing five different doctors and nurse practitioners. Her diagnoses ranged from teething to digestion problems, but no treatment they suggested seemed to make Adalyn feel any better.

Having been a nurse for thirteen years, I knew something was wrong. Finally, at the start of the third week of nonstop pain and sleepless nights, I called and requested every test possible.

The blood work looked bad, but the CT scan was worse. And when they told me that Adalyn's pediatrician had broken off his vacation to come and talk to us, I knew that whatever they found was worse than I could have imagined. Even so, nothing could have prepared me for the words, *Adalyn has a mass in her pelvis.* It was a possible tumor, and they needed to transfer her to another hospital for further treatment.

I remembered how I had written on Facebook about trusting God, how I wanted "His will above all else." At the time I had thought it meant regarding finances or my marriage, but not this, not little Adalyn. I scrambled to pull the words back, telling God that this was not what I wanted. "How can this be Your will, God?" I prayed.

It was only when a friend came to visit that I started to calm down. She grabbed my hand and looked hard at me. "Kim," she said, "what is her middle name?"

"Faith," I said.

"God told you to name her Faith for this very day because that is what you need! Faith!"

I cried myself to sleep that night, Adalyn curled up in my arms. I woke often, each time thinking that it was all a bad dream, only for the bleeping of the IV to remind me that this was all very much real.

The two-hour ride to Shreveport was grueling. Adalyn could not sit in her car seat because the mass pushed all her organs out of place and was too painful, so I sat in the back with her while she slept in my arms. As we drove, I told God exactly what I thought about it all. I was mad. I told Him that I didn't understand why this was happening. Eventually my words ran dry, and I listened to the playlist I had made. Songs such as "When I Don't Know What to Do," "Praise You in This Storm," and "Never Once" filled the car, and I sang, cried, and prayed along with them. In time I realized that the God I was singing to and ranting at was the same God I had praised a week before when I did not know Adalyn was sick. My circumstances had changed, but He had not. His love for me was solid, unconditional. Was mine for Him the same?

Somewhere between Alexandria and Shreveport, I turned it over to Him. I told God that no matter what the outcome, I would praise Him. I would have faith that His will was pleasing and perfect and that I didn't have to understand it to trust it. I told Him that I really did desire His will above all else. And from that moment on, I had peace.

The tests and procedures began on Friday. All weekend they filled her with antibiotics while we waited and prayed. The doctors were such godly people, and before taking Adalyn in to surgery, the surgeon asked if we could pray together. I knew God had sent him to take care of my baby, and even though I felt helpless and out of control, I knew that God was with me and He was more than enough.

After five hours in surgery, the doctor emerged.

"There's no cancer," he said. "All we could find in the mass was an infection." He went on to explain that what the CT scan had shown and what he had found were two different things entirely, and in the days that followed, some of the best pathologists in the country were sent samples. One by one they all agreed that there was no cancer in our little girl.

To me, it was a miracle, and a nurse told me the doctors were calling it "an act of God."

I needed what little faith I had in order to get through it all, but I also know that I have emerged stronger and bolder in my belief in God. These days when I pray "Your will above all else," I know that I mean it!

37

Obeying God

Nicole Waltamath

I so wanted to become a wife and mother. To me, it was a God-given desire, and having been in a relationship for four years, the last two of them engaged, I was sure that it was about to happen.

But I was also starting to wonder about things. My fiancé and I had a lot of problems, and we fought constantly. The negatives were outnumbering the positives, and it was starting to nag at my thoughts. And even though somewhere in the back of my head I knew that God didn't want me in this relationship, I was deliberately ignoring God's will for me.

And then I had the dream. It wasn't complicated, but when I woke up I felt taken aback. In my dream I had seen a man standing in front of a black background, a spotlight shining on him. The strangest thing was that I knew this man; he was a friend of mine from a few years back, but I hadn't seen him or spoken to him in years. Something inside of me felt such joy from having this dream, and joy wasn't something I experienced a lot of with my fiancé.

After a few days I completely forgot about the dream, but it must have made an impression on me because within a couple of weeks I decided to end my two-year engagement. It was a very hard decision to make, and I desperately didn't want to hurt my fiancé. But as soon as I ended it, I felt a sense of freedom that had been missing for too long. Finally I felt that I was stepping back onto God's path for me.

While out shopping a month or two after that, I was talking to the cashier who was a friend of mine from a few years back. She wanted to know how I was and how things were going with my fiancé and me.

"I don't know how he is," I said. "We broke up." As soon as I said those words, the dream that I had forgotten about came right back to me. But that wasn't all; the girl I was talking to was actually the sister of the man in my dream. Still, I was just out of a four-year relationship and didn't want to go chasing fantasies, so I quickly pushed any thoughts of the dream away.

But the story doesn't end there. A little while after I talked with his sister, the guy in the dream reached out to me and asked me out on our first date. This man became the love of my life. He made me his wife, and one day soon I hope to be the mother of his children.

I believe that God gave me that dream to save me from taking a road and life that He didn't want me to have. I believe God stepped in and intervened in my marriage because God cares about marriage. And I believe that when we let God in and listen—when we let Him have control—He will do amazing things in our lives. We just have to open our eyes, let Him into our dreams, and be ready to take a risk.

38

Responding to the Spirit

Suzanne Blomquist

My son and daughter were away for the weekend, visiting their dad. He lived in a different part of town, and I was at home, not really doing much. It was around 11:00 a.m. when, for no reason at all, I suddenly had a strong urge to get in the car and drive down Sprague Avenue. I rarely went over to that side of town, except to drop the children off at their father's. Still, I couldn't shake the feeling that I needed to head over that way, so I got in the car and drove.

Sprague can get pretty busy in places, and as I made my way along the five-lane stretch, I was shocked to see a little boy all alone on the street corner. He was wearing a pair of shorts and no shoes, and by the way he covered his face, I guessed he was crying. I was so disturbed by the sight of him that I knew I had to turn around and find out why he was alone and how I could help.

As I pulled my car in close to him, the little boy turned

toward me. It was my nine-year-old son, Dana. I can't begin to describe the sense of horror that flooded me in that moment, and I ran from the car as fast as I could.

In between the tears that flowed from both of us, Dana told me what had happened. He explained that his dad and sister had gone to the store, but he hadn't wanted to go, so he had been allowed to stay home as long as he stayed in the house until they returned. Everything was fine until a bird hit the window. Dana went outside to see if the bird was okay, and when he tried to go back into the house, he found that the door had self-locked, and he was unable to get in.

Dana had decided that the best thing he could do was go to the gas station down the block to call me and have me come over and help him. Only he hadn't quite realized what a big road he had to cross to get to the gas station. And then, just when he was really starting to panic, he looked up to see me.

The tears kept coming for both of us. The story could have had many horrible endings, but instead of leaving me gripped by fear, I felt that I was the most blessed person in the world that day. God had spoken to me, and I had been able to listen. From that day on I have always paid attention to what I feel God is telling me—whether it's loud and clear, a still, small voice, or just a hunch that I need to be somewhere else. God's messages come in all kinds of ways.

39

The Bridge

David Ridilla

I was a healthy forty-five-year-old husband and father of the three most wonderful children God has ever placed on earth: Brianna was fourteen, Adam was twelve, and Maria was ten years old. The only trouble was, I had cancer.

My wife, Karen, and I had decided not to make a big deal about my diagnosis around the children. Every evening when we said family prayers, the kids would pray for me, and I would pray for wisdom and direction, but to avoid scaring the kids, I didn't go into a lot of detail.

Those first weeks that followed the leukemia diagnosis in April 2008 were hard. I felt as though I had been hit by a train and knew that I had to find a doctor who could cure me so I could continue to be there for my family and provide for them. For a while I felt God had abandoned me, but my pastor helped get me back to a positive frame of mind and out of the "blaming God" stage. My wife and I visited many doctors in the Pittsburgh area but just didn't seem to find what we were looking for, so we widened our search. After researching doctors who specialize in chronic lymphocytic leukemia, we felt there were two leaders in the field: one in New York and the other in Texas. New York was closer, so a month after my diagnosis we headed north.

The doctor ran tests and told me that he wanted to take a conservative approach and not start treatment yet. At first I felt okay with this, but after returning home and as the days wore on, my initial peace and confidence began to fade. Soon I was wondering whether I should also make a trip down to Texas for a second opinion. I prayed daily for wisdom.

In June 2008, while we were still trying to decide if we should travel to Texas, I went on a weeklong hike on the C&O Canal between Washington DC, and Cumberland, Maryland, with my son, Adam, and his Boy Scout troop.

On the third day of the hike, Adam asked if Mom and I had made a decision on whether we were going to see the doctor in Texas. We were in the middle of a twelve-mile stretch that day, carrying full backpacks containing everything we needed to survive for the whole week. We were hot, tired, and sore. I had two blisters on each foot, but the conversation with Adam is what really stands out in my memory. I told him that we hadn't decided yet but were still looking into it. After a lengthy discussion about why I should or shouldn't go, Adam paused and asked, "How are you going to make a decision?"

I thought about it. "God will guide us in the right direction," I said.

"How will you know?"

"Well," I said, "He will put something in my life that will make me feel at peace. It might be something I read, someone I talk to, or maybe nothing significant but just peace through prayer."

Adam thought awhile before he spoke next. "When?"

"When it's the right time for God," I said. "I'm in no hurry, Adam."

"Is this why you pray for wisdom and direction every night?"

"Mostly."

"Dad," Adam said, "when we say our prayers in our tent tonight, I am going to pray for you to get better like I always do, but I am also going to pray that God gives you a sign."

"Thanks, buddy," I said. "I really appreciate it."

While in the tent later that evening, we read scripture from my pocket Bible and said our evening prayers. Adam focused on God helping me make a decision on whether we should travel to Texas or not, and I remember the exact words that he prayed: ". . . and God please give my dad a sign on what he should do so nothing bad happens to him . . ." We finished up with scripture, blessed each other, and went to sleep.

The next day I left early with a few boys, Adam included. It was due to get as hot as ninety-five degrees with high humidity, so I was glad to be leaving early. After getting up at 5:50, eating breakfast, tearing down the tent, and loading our backpacks, I was on the trail at 6:30 with Adam and three of his buddies.

A half-hour in, we approached an access bridge. Just past it we saw a middle-aged couple walking toward us, and as we met at the end of the bridge, the couple turned around and started walking with us. The gentleman explained that every morning before work, he and his wife walked to the bridge and back to the car park.

His wife, in a very motherly manner, started talking to Adam and his friends while the husband and I had a conversation about the canal, Boy Scouts, wildlife, and more. At some point he mentioned that he had a patient who backpacked the canal on a regular basis. It struck me as interesting, and when there was a lull in the conversation, I said, "You mentioned awhile back that you have a patient who hikes the canal. I take it that you're a doctor?"

"Yes," he said. "I'm a hematologist."

I smiled. "That's funny. I've been seeing a lot of you guys lately."

He turned his head quickly toward me. "Hopefully nothing serious," he said.

I told him I had been diagnosed in April with chronic lymphocytic leukemia. As the words came out of my mouth, I sensed the hair on the back of my neck standing up and chills starting to run down my back.

For thirty minutes we talked. He told me that he was the chief clinical transplant hematologist at Georgetown University Hospital in Washington DC. I told him my medical history, my blood counts, and more. I explained that I wasn't happy with the doctors around home and that I had traveled to New York to see a specialist. He knew of the doctor I had seen, and we talked extensively about my doctor's decision not to start treatment yet.

When I told him that I was considering a visit down

to Texas, he looked puzzled. "Why would you consider the trip?" he asked. I gave him my reasons, which suddenly didn't sound quite as strong as they previously had. With a confidence in his voice that was infectious, he told me that he felt a trip to Texas would be a waste of my time at this point. He assured me that both doctors were wonderful but encouraged me to hold off a trip to Texas for a while.

I was amazed! The fact that Adam's prayer had been answered so quickly and with such clarity had me flooded with thanks to God. It was so wonderful that He would put this doctor in my life at that very moment, allowing not just my son's prayer to be answered but mine and my wife's too.

As we were saying our good-byes, I thanked the doctor for his time and willingness to share his opinions. Then I said, "God does answer prayers." He looked at me with a somewhat puzzled expression on his face. So I just shook his hand and said, "You will never know how much you just helped me. Thank you and have a great day."

As we walked away, Adam ran over to me, and we discussed what had just happened. He told me that he had been trying to listen to my conversation with the doctor while still being polite and participating in his conversation with the doctor's wife at the same time, but he knew that something special had just happened.

Six years on from my diagnosis, I still have not started any treatments. The doctor from New York is now eighty-two years old and three years ago transferred my care to his colleague in Columbus, Ohio. My new doctor is following the same conservative plan and tells me that when the time comes for me to need treatment, it will be with the new medications that are just being approved, not with chemotherapy. I praise God for that.

My health? Well, that's been pretty good. I know my limits, and we have adjusted well to the "new normal." That means spending more time together as a family and less time running in circles.

The incident made an impact on Adam too. Just one year after hiking the C&O Canal, he received scouting's highest ranking of Eagle at just thirteen years old. He's planning on attending the University of Pittsburgh at Johnstown to major in civil engineering. What can I say . . . the boy likes bridges!

Thanks to the God thing of Adam's answered prayer and the meeting with the doctor on the bridge, I have been able to be there for my family. Life is good, God is great, and I am a very blessed man!

40

Miracle on the High Seas

Phuong Schuetz

Some people have told me that I'm lucky. They hear my story, open their eyes wide, shake their heads, and try to tell me the only reason I have survived this far is because of a series of happy coincidences. They couldn't be more wrong.

It all started with the end of the Vietnam War. My homeland was a desperate place in which to live in those days, especially once Saigon fell to communism on April 30, 1975. That was when my father was imprisoned, and my family lost both our freedom and our livelihood. My dad was sent to one of the communist re-education camps, along with other Vietnamese men and American POWs. It was a desperate place to be, but somehow my dad survived, and in 1978, he was released.

I was nine years old at the time, and I knew little of the great exodus of people fleeing the country. I didn't know then that the rest of the world was watching, referring to these refugees as boat people, and I certainly didn't know that I was about to become one of them. Yet my parents knew that if we were going to survive, we had to get out.

Fleeing the communist state of Vietnam was not easy. It was dangerous, expensive, and illegal. My aunt paid gold to a fisherman in the village of Chu Hai in order to secure a place on the boat for all seven of our family members. Over the course of three nights at the end of May 1979, each of us was transported separately, with only a few personal belongings, from our home in Saigon to the boat owner's home in the fishing village along the coast.

We were kept apart from one another until the third night. There was no moon to guide us as we ran barefoot across marshes and rice paddies to reach the fishing boat, and once on board all of us had to go below deck in the boat's storage area until dawn when we were safely out of the borders of Vietnam.

We weren't alone on the boat. There were thirty-five adults and seven children tightly packed onto the 36 by 42-foot wooden fishing boat. There was no protection from the sun that burned overhead, and all of us shared the same fear of the unknown. To make matters worse, my mother was six months pregnant. There was talk of Thai pirates who preyed on boats like ours, stealing what little possessions those on board had brought with them, often assaulting, kidnapping, and even killing their victims. The best we could hope for was being quickly rescued at sea or finding our way to safer shores.

Two days into the journey, word went around the boat that the crew had no compass with them. They had no radio or any other means of navigation. We were lost, and there was nothing we could do about it. Nothing, that is, except pray. My grandmother and others on the boat began praying fervently. "God is our compass," they said.

When day four came around, we were down to our last portions of food, water, and fuel. Each of us was given only small bites of food and small sips of water and, with no room to move about, we simply sat in our places, scorched each day by the blazing sun. When our thirst became unbearable, we scooped up the ocean water to drink, even though we knew that it would only leave us thirsting for more. It was cooler at night, at least, but the fierce winds and rainstorms whipped our flimsy boat every which way as we hung on to each other for dear life. Had God's hedge of protection not been around that little wooden boat, our lives would not have been spared.

Miraculously, everyone on our boat survived the first week. And then, on the eighth day, we saw a boat approaching. As it neared us, it became clear that this was no rescue ship but, instead, one of the dreaded Thai pirate ships that trawled the waters like sharks.

They boarded our boat, but strangely they didn't seem intent on assaulting, killing, or even robbing us. Instead, they wanted to trade. In exchange for our jewels and valuables, the pirates actually gave us food, water, fuel, and directions before sending us on our way. Three days later our little boat, CH 25, was granted permission to come ashore at a small refugee camp in Tioman, Malaysia.

We stayed on the island for two months before being transferred to a bigger camp in Malaysia. After living there for seven months, our family was sponsored by St. Matthew's Lutheran Church in Erie, Pennsylvania, and on February 29, 1980, we made it to our new permanent home.

Each time I retell this story, I am more amazed at how God was involved in every aspect of our journey from the very beginning. My dad survived and was released from prison. None of us got separated during the escape. During the run to the boat, we were not caught. We survived daytime heat, nighttime storms, limited rations, and the risk of malnutrition, and came out of our meeting with the Thai pirates unharmed. My mother even went on to give birth to a healthy daughter. And throughout it all God kept our family intact.

How could all this be considered luck? How could it simply be a coincidence? So many of my countrymen and women died while trying to make the crossing, and many lived in refugee camps for years before being sent back to Vietnam; yet God rescued us from all those circumstances. Because God had mercy on us, my family escaped successfully on our first attempt while so many others didn't.

I believe that God saved us for a reason. He saved us because He had a plan for our lives, for my life. That's why He rescued me—so that I can keep on telling His story through articles and blogs and every way possible. I want to help people find hope, love, and truth in a life with Jesus.

When you're talking about the God of the universe who still performs miracles, who displays His might and power in order to reveal Himself to people who do not yet know Him, luck has nothing to do with it.

41

A Changed Life

Peggy Tippin

I died. But my story did not end there. Even though my heart stopped beating and I was considered brain-dead, it wasn't the end. God wasn't finished with me yet.

It all happened one morning: Apart from waking up, taking a shower, getting my clothes and makeup on, and leaving for work, there's not much that I remember about January 22, 2013. I arrived at my job as director of student services by 8:00 a.m. and set about all the tasks stacked up in front of me. It was the first day back to classes for students at the college, and I had a lot to do. It was definitely not the kind of day you want to get up from your desk sometime around 11:00 a.m., walk down the hallway, start to limp, have your skin turn purple, and fall down dead.

That's what I did, though. My heart stopped beating, and I lay on the floor. One of the nurses at the college started CPR on me, and she was joined by the career services director.

They handed me over to the emergency response personnel who continued trying to revive me for another thirty minutes.

Six times the doctors shocked me with a defibrillator in a desperate attempt to get my heart beating again. Nothing worked. And when I had reached forty-five minutes without any blood getting to my brain, my prognosis was bleak. The neurologist was asked to come down and see how bad the damage was. He could find no brain waves. I didn't respond to stimuli, there was no pupil dilation, no movement in my arms and legs, and no gag reflex. I was brain-dead.

But the neurologist had an idea. He told my family about one last treatment that he could try: therapeutic hypothermia. When the brain doesn't receive oxygen, it begins producing a toxin and self-destructs, causing brain damage. The way to stop the toxin production is to cool the body. He wanted to inject my veins with iced saline to bring my body temperature down to ninety-one degrees Fahrenheit (thirty-three degrees Celsius).

This procedure, however, is usually carried out within twenty to thirty minutes of the heart stopping, not forty-five, as it was in my case. If this was going to work, it would be one of the longest periods from which the doctor and his team had seen a patient come back.

My family agreed, and just twelve hours into the procedure—which normally takes anywhere from twenty-four to forty-eight hours—the doctor allowed the paralytic drug that stops patients from shivering to wear off. Within a few hours, and with tubes still running down my throat, I woke up.

I had studied sign language many years earlier and had been just one class away from my interpreter's license. Even though I had not studied it since I became pregnant with my last child—twenty-two years before—it was to sign language that I returned as I lay shivering and full of tubes in the hospital room. "Why am I so cold?" I asked.

Three days later my memory began to clear, and I started returning to my normal self. Doctors diagnosed me with heart arrhythmia, which had momentarily stopped my heart. To prevent that from happening again, I was given an internal defibrillator, and I returned to work, living my normal life just three weeks after I was believed to be clinically dead.

Coming back to life changed me. It gave me a renewed sense of faith and a renewed sense of perspective. The things I thought were a big deal are no longer big deals, and I have seen a change in my priorities. I realized that life is a gift, and I am going to live it that way. And I know more than ever that God is in control of my life. He's the one who gave me my life back. He's the one I'm living for. He's the one who was in complete and total control. And He still is.

42

Saved

Michaela Sandeno

I have been a swimmer for eleven years. I've spent so much time in the pool that there have been days when I've talked to my dad about quitting, thinking that doing so would mean being able to spend more time with God. But every time I have brought it up, my dad has always said the same thing: "God has you swimming for a reason." On Friday, June 29, 2013, I found out how right he was.

My family was driving up to Minnesota from Parker, Colorado. We were going to spend the Fourth of July with our cousins at Ethel Beach, stopping off on the way at an Indian reservation in South Dakota to pick up my younger brother, David.

It took awhile before my parents, my sisters, and I found David. He was with his church group, hanging out on the beach and having fun at the end of their mission trip. It must have been ninety degrees outside, so the lake looked inviting.

When David and a few of the others decided to swim back to the parking lot, instead of walking the long way around, I said I would join them—anything to cool down.

Even though it was a hot day, the water was cold. Almost halfway across, LJ—one of the leaders—said he wanted to go back. The whole group stopped and another leader said, "LJ, we're almost there. It's not that far, you can finish."

"No," said LJ. "I've got to go back."

Everyone in the youth ministry knew that I was a swimmer, so while they kept swimming across, LJ yelled out to me to help him get back to the shore.

"You can make it by yourself," I said. "And I have to get back across with David. We've got a lot more driving to do."

I started swimming away, but LJ yelled out. "Michaela, I can't see anything. Everything's black, and my limbs are numb."

My legs were cold, too, but I swam the six feet over to him, just as LJ bobbed under the water. He wasn't just panicking about nothing—there really was something wrong.

I grabbed his arm and held him up, treading water as best I could. I've treaded water before at swim practice but never while trying to stop a 170-pound man from sinking. The cold water made it even more difficult because my legs were already numb. I don't think I've ever prayed harder.

I had to keep telling LJ, "Don't keep pulling down on my arm, or we are both going to drown."

Every time I said that, he responded with, "I'm not," but still he continued to push down harder and harder. I told him to pray. "Believe me, I am!" he said.

I had been yelling for help since LJ first went under, but

nobody had come yet. I prayed and prayed and prayed that LJ would miraculously get better and that we would be able to make it back to the beach, or that someone would come with a boat to pick us up. Strangely, though I don't think I've ever been so scared that I was going to die, something deep inside told me it was okay, and I was able to stay calm—for most of the time at least.

After what seemed like half an hour, but was probably only fifteen minutes, an older couple in a boat came within shouting range, and I screamed, "Help!" in their direction. They changed their course and headed right toward us. After they had safely lifted LJ into their boat, they asked if I wanted a ride back to the beach, too, but I said no. I needed some time by myself to talk to God and thank Him for saving LJ from drowning and for keeping me safe from LJ and his panic to stay afloat.

When I got back to shore, however, and saw LJ safe on dry land, I looked for the boat and the couple who had helped me, but I couldn't find them anywhere, or their boat. I know for a fact that the boat did not pass me leaving the beach—it was as though it just disappeared. With the time that has passed, both LJ and I believe that God answered our prayers and we entertained angels unaware that day.

43

All Things New

Amanda Bosarge

Sometimes you just have to drop your pride in order for God to do what He wants. And sometimes, just when you think you've been humbled enough, God asks you to drop just a little more before He unleashes His blessings. At least, that's how it happened with me.

It began as an ordinary day. I woke up and began dressing the children. Everything was peachy until I tried to get up from my daughter's bed. All of a sudden I couldn't move. I tried to stand again, but my back would not straighten. I had no idea what to do, so I waited awhile.

Now, I am twenty-five years young, and I really believe in good health. That's why I was seeing a chiropractor at the time—to help me maintain a healthy spine.

A few minutes later I picked up my baby to try to change her diaper. I just about made it to the hallway before I collapsed. That's when I knew this was serious and I needed help.

I hobbled to my neighbor's house to get help. Thankfully I already had an appointment with my chiropractor scheduled for that morning, so my neighbor helped me load up my children. "Lord," I prayed as she buckled them in and I tried to hold back the signs of just how excruciating the pain had become, "please help Dr. Mike fix me."

When I reached the office, the staff unloaded my children while I half-crawled to the adjustment table. Dr. Mike happens to be one of the best chiropractors around, and I was sure that, at the very least, he would be able to ease my pain. After almost two hours with him, I began to lose hope. He tried everything to ease the pain but to no avail. What was worse was the fact that everyone else seemed to be alarmed at my condition. I asked whether it would fix itself anytime soon and felt my heart sink when he told me that this could last for a month or more before I received any relief.

My prayers had changed by this point. I had started to tell God that I trusted Him, that I knew He had allowed me to be inflicted with this for a reason. But I wanted to be healed more than ever.

When my husband came home from work that day, he was worried at the sight of me hunched over and limping. And no matter how hard I tried, I could not right myself. I was in constant, intense pain, and I couldn't sit, stand, or lie down. If I wanted to get anywhere around the house, most of the time I just crawled.

By the time the weekend came, I was no better. I had to attend a church class Saturday morning and was forced to take notes on my hands and knees. My disability was so obvious, and I started to feel that I understood a little of what it feels like to be crippled. At the end of class, believers came and laid hands on me, and though I was thankful for all the help, and I desperately wanted to be healed, it wasn't God's timing. Once I realized this, all I wanted to do was get home.

I needed a miracle, fast. My husband works out of town during the week, and he was not going to be home to help me with the children come Sunday afternoon. So when Sunday morning came, I hobbled into church and asked people to pray for me. They laid hands on me and prayed earnestly for God to heal me. When everyone went back to their seats, I was still hunched over. I began to pray again. "What should I do next, Lord?" I asked. Somehow I knew His answer: get up and walk around the sanctuary seven times.

I hesitated for a while. Was I sure that was Him? Finally I chose to obey. I began to walk the first lap and continued to pray as I hobbled along. Every lap I made, my faith grew. As I walked, bit by bit I could feel my back start to release, and by the seventh lap, I could stand up straight with no pain at all.

I was overwhelmed at the miracle I had just experienced in my own body, overwhelmed with my miracle healing. Right then and there I began to testify to the congregation what had just happened. We were all rejoicing, and it was a beautiful moment I will never forget.

I went back to my seat and sat straighter than I had ever sat before. The next week I made my weekly visit to Dr. Mike. Normally my back would pop all over during the adjustment while he realigned my spine, but at this visit nothing popped at all!

"Why's that?" I asked.

"Your back is perfectly aligned," he said.

God didn't just heal my infirmity; He completely fixed my entire spine. How great a God thing is that?

44

The Key

Barbara Thompson

The last load was in the pickup. I stood in the empty living room. It didn't just sound echoey and strange; it felt as though we had already left. I took one final look around the house that had been our home for the last three and a half years—the marks on the floor where our plants had stood on either side of the fireplace, the bare wood floors and white walls, and the empty backyard all told me the same thing: there was nothing left to do. It was time to go.

My son and I had moved into this house just before he started kindergarten. A lot had happened in the few years we had been there, and we had both made a lot of new friends in the neighborhood. But I had decided to go back to school, so we were moving in with my mother, not just to save money or so she could help me with my son, but I also wanted to help her with my grandmother.

I locked the front door, and my son and I got into the

pickup, ready for the ten-mile drive to Mom's house. I felt in my pocket for the truck key but couldn't find it. I distinctly remembered putting it there, and since it was the only key I had, it was imperative I find it. I searched and emptied my pockets multiple times but no key. I did the same with my purse, then the cab of the truck, but again the same result: no key. We went back into the house to look and then searched the yard. I looked in my pockets again, certain I had put it there. No key.

It was getting dark, so I told my son we would have to sleep on the floor that night in order to get him to school in the morning. Luckily we had loaded our bedding and clothes last, and after eating at a nearby restaurant that was within walking distance, we slept well enough on the floor of our old home.

Not having an alarm clock, we were late waking up the next day. I walked my son to his elementary school, but on the way as we passed a side street, I thought I heard a faint call for help. We stopped. I heard it again. We went to investigate. A heavyset elderly woman sat on the cement walkway in front of her house with her large legs splayed out in front of her.

"What happened?" I asked.

"I was on my way to Bible study when I fell. Could you help me up, please?"

In the past I had worked as a nurse's aide, and my first job was in a nursing home, where I had received training in body mechanics and gained five years of experience lifting people. I asked her if she thought she might have injured anything, asking particularly about her hips. "I don't think I'm injured," she said. "I fall like this all the time. Do you think you can help me get up?"

She seemed coherent, so I got behind her, had her cross her arms in front of her, and grasped her wrists from behind. Using my legs, I lifted her to her feet. She made it to her feet, thanked me profusely, and, with a waddling gait, hurried to her car and drove away.

My son and I retraced our steps and resumed walking to school. It struck me that this was a teachable moment, so I told my son, "I would not be surprised if God set this whole thing up so that we could be there to help that lady. Think about it: we lost the key, had the bedding all ready to go but no alarm clock, and we got here at exactly the right time. And that woman was heavy, and I guess I was the one person around here who knew how to lift her. Coincidence? I'll bet I could reach in my pocket right now and find the key." As I said this, I reached into my pocket and felt the key to the truck. I pulled it out and showed him.

My son is a grown man now, but I'll never forget that incident. It was as if God had given me a glimpse, at the very end of our time in the neighborhood, of how He loves us, cares for us, and wants to weave us into His plans to help others.

45

Touched by God

Cathy Rueff

I guess everybody has seasons where life just seems hard. For me, it was August 2006. My husband had undergone surgery for a knee injury, which led to a staph infection and three further surgeries. Surely nothing else could go wrong, could it?

That's when I developed a stabbing pain in my right side. My doctor thought it was a virus, and then he thought it was an infection, but he advised me to go to the emergency room if the pain got worse. It got worse.

The doctors who examined me decided I should have my appendix removed, but after the next day's surgery, they informed me that there really was nothing wrong with my appendix, though they took it out anyway. My family physician ordered a CT scan, which showed nothing. A gynecologist said that since I'd had a hysterectomy years before, there was nothing he could do. Another doctor ordered a colonoscopy, but again he found nothing. All he could suggest was more pain meds and another CT scan. A surgical specialist took a look, ordered two MRIs, and found arthritis in my spine but no reason for the relentless pain in my side.

That's when a couple at church told me that I needed to be anointed.

"No way," I said. "Anointing is for when you're on your death bed or something."

They disagreed and reminded me of what it says in James 5:14: anyone who is sick should call the elders and have them pray for and anoint him or her with oil. So I agreed.

The morning before they were due to come over to pray and anoint me with oil, I prayed. I gave everything I could possibly think of to God. When my pastor and the elders arrived, I carried on praying, surrendering to God. They put oil on my forehead and placed a Bible on my side where the pain was. During the prayer, I felt heat go from my shoulder to my side and something like a baby kick inside me. By the time they finished and I stood up, I was totally pain-free.

That was April 17, 2007, and I have been pain-free ever since. God touched me and healed me that day in a way that only He could.

I began telling my story to people, giving God the glory for what He had done. Soon I was asked to speak at local churches and even at a women's retreat consisting of at least three churches. I had never been one to get up and speak in front of a crowd—just four years prior to this, I had lost a job for not being assertive—so being able to speak to these people had to have been from God.

The greatest thing was that after each time I shared what God had done for me, several people came up to share with me what God had done for them. I was so blessed by their stories, and it strengthened my faith all the more. In sharing my own story and listening to others', I have been constantly reminded that God can—and does—use the hard aspects of our lives as well as the good ones to reveal His glory.

There are so many people whose lives are being touched by God on a daily basis. We need to tell these stories and encourage each other with them because God is alive today. Let's make sure our stories are heard, shall we?

46

The Wisdom of a Son

Diane Belz

It had been a day of torture. From the minute I woke up, all throughout my workday and even for the hour spent in my spin class, I had felt tortured, tormented, and torn apart. As I was heading back home from the gym, my mind replayed the thoughts that had been building for a while. *You are better than him. You deserve more than he's giving you. You've gotta leave him, or else this torture will never end.* No matter what I did, I could not stop those words from shouting at me. So rather than fight them, I decided to give in. I decided that this was going to be the day that I would deal with the problem fully. I had put it off for too long, enough with the delays. Today was the day that I would walk out on my husband. Tonight I would put twenty-three years of marriage behind me and go off in search of a better life.

I arrived home and encountered my youngest son, fifteen-year-old Geoff. He was home alone because my husband was out with his friends, of course. Geoff knew I was at the end of my rope, and I knew that Geoff would want me to stay. But what could I do? My marriage to his father was over.

As I was headed up the stairs to pack my bags, he asked, "Are you leaving us tonight?"

"Yes," I answered. It was a pathetic thing for a mother to say to her son, but it was all I could do.

"Can you do me a favor?" Geoff asked.

A favor? What was he talking about? But instead of brushing him off, I just said, "What?"

I was expecting him to ask me to take him with me or to stay or to give it one more chance if he promised to behave. But he didn't say any of those things. Instead, he asked, "Can you take a bath?" It didn't make any sense.

"Why a bath?" I asked.

"When we were little and you had had enough of us, you would escape and take a bath. It would always make you feel better. So can you just take a bath for me? I want you to feel better."

How many times have you had to prompt your kids into the bath or shower? For me and my two very active boys, it felt like a million times. How many times had they asked me to do the same? Never. This was a first for me and, hopefully, the last. For whatever reason, I said yes. Once I'd had the bath, I would be out of there before my husband came home.

My son was right; the bathtub was my place of solace and relaxation. In agreeing to his request, I was saying yes to my desire to be taken away from all this torment. The bathtub had been the vessel that I used to travel across time and space as I read countless romance novels and women's magazines, all the while soaking away until the hot water went cold. I wanted to be taken to one of those places again, where the hero loves the heroine and there are no money problems or children with challenges. I wanted to go to a place where love is undying and peace reigns.

This was an important bath, and because of it I needed to find a good book. While the tub filled up, my search for reading material took me into my office. There I saw the bag my best friend had left me the night before. She knew how I was feeling, how painful our marriage had become, and she had asked if she could drop off a gift. She is a great gift giver, and at the time she was the only one who was putting anything into the positive column in my life. I hadn't looked in the Victoria's Secret bag when it arrived, and my expectations were high as I picked it up. What would she have bought me? Candy? Bath beads? A sexy nightie for my new life to come, or a good book?

It was none of the first three. But it was a book. In fact, there were two books, both of them not at all what I was expecting. I pulled them out of the bag and stared at them. What was she thinking? In one hand I held a big, fat, pink Bible while in the other was a little book titled *How to Save Your Marriage Alone*. Great. Just what I needed—a book about doing it alone. Wasn't isolation the root of the problem in the first place? How could it help at all?

As for the Bible, I was the kind of woman who thought that a big bottle of wine was a better choice for solving my troubles. I decided to keep looking in the bag, as though it was my Christmas stocking, hoping that some really special trinket was hidden, tucked deep inside. Nope. Just the two books. Maybe she wasn't such a great gift giver after all.

For some reason the thought of bringing the Bible into the tub evoked visions of me burning in liquid fire as the sacred tome touched the water. For safety's sake I opted for the little book and left the Good Book in the bag.

The little book, I quickly discovered, was a page-turner. The intrigue mounted as I discovered to my utter amazement how wretched a wife I had become. And, just as I had hoped, this book did transport me back in time. I read about Jesus and the meaning of true love. I read about the apostles Peter and Paul and love being patient, and wives submitting to their husbands. Rather than being repulsed and revolted by the words, I felt repulsed and revolted by the revelation of how I had been living.

I felt disgusted with myself. I felt unclean. All my harsh words, all my disrespect, the withholding of love and affection . . . it all crowded into my head and heart. I felt as if I were drowning, yet my head wasn't even underneath the water. My sins were taking me down, and I wanted to be made clean. There was not a drug or drink that could quench the hunger I had for forgiveness, but from whom could I ask for it?

But ask I did. Not to be forgiven by my husband or children but to be forgiven by the One I had sinned most greatly against, my Father. I begged God to forgive me and, if possible, to take away all the anger and hurt I was feeling. I then did the unthinkable: I made a pact with God. If He would forgive me, I would become a godly woman.

It was a desperate prayer from a desperate woman. I put my head under the spigot to rinse my hair, pleading and sobbing as I hung my head in shame. I asked God to take away the pain of my sins and the anger I felt toward my husband. If God forgave me, then I could learn how to forgive my husband and myself.

What I received was unexpected. Unlike with my son's request and my friend's gift, I couldn't guess what God was going to do next, but what happened was instantaneous. He released me. Not over time, not over weeks and months. He did it then and there. As I wept tears, asking for forgiveness, as the water washed over me, I felt God pull the weight of all my sins away from me. He lifted the burden, and I felt light, free, finally unchained from the person I had become.

Fear soon started to come over me. Did I say the right words? Was I even allowed to be making pacts with God? What if I let Him down? Would this feeling of forgiveness last if I left the tub? The cold water silenced all those voices, reminding me whom I had become—a born-again, beloved daughter of God.

After rising from the tub and drying off my wet but now very clean heart, mind, body, and soul, I dressed and walked out my bedroom door. I was not carrying the suitcase as I had thought I would. I was not carrying anything. For the first time in a long time, I had no sinful baggage.

As I floated down the steps, my son was standing at the landing, waiting for me. What he said confirmed all that I felt. "The woman who went up those stairs is not the same woman who came down. Everything is going to be okay."

His words were a hopeful and prophetic declaration that all was well. And I knew it too. The God who created the universe, parted the Red Sea, filled empty wombs, and caused empty tombs had healed my broken heart. Did I look any different? I didn't know. I knew for sure, though, that I was different. My bathtub baptism had changed everything.

If this were the end of the story, it would be a very good ending. But it is not the end. The Lord knew that my marriage struggles were not the only challenges in my path as six months later our daughter died suddenly. Without my bathtub miracle I believe that the lives of our four remaining family members would have been destroyed. Yet God knew the plans He had for us, plans to prosper us and not to harm us, plans to give us hope and a future (Jer. 29:11 NIV). And He did all this in the bathtub.

47

That's What God Can Do

Lorie Chaffin

After she had been diagnosed with lung cancer, it took only three weeks for my mother to pass away. Yet despite the pain of a rapid ending, she never once questioned, doubted, or cried during those twenty-one days. She was at complete peace.

So many times my mom told me that she would show me what God can do. And so many times she did; she showed me how God can bring peace and how God can be found in the middle of suffering. Most of all she showed me what being a Christian is truly about.

Several years after she passed away, I was flicking through her old Bible. I liked looking at the pages, spotting the passages that she had circled or annotated. But when I got to John 9:31, there was one note that stood out from all the others. In her familiar hand she had written in the margin, "God's promise for John." You see, John is my dad, and he was about as lost as a person can be. It was exciting to know that Mom thought this verse was significant: "We know that God does not listen to sinners, but if anyone is a worshiper of God and does his will, God listens to him" (ESV).

Fast-forward to the fall of 2011, when cancer returned to my family's everyday vocabulary. My dad was diagnosed with stage three rectal cancer with lymph node involvement. The doctor who found the cancer said that my dad needed to get specialized treatment, so he traveled to the University of Kentucky Hospital in Lexington, Kentucky, to begin the process.

With a colorectal specialist in Lexington and other doctors in our hometown, Dad went through chemotherapy, radiation, scans, tests, and more. My dad and I made many trips to the various doctors for all these treatments, and during those trips, I played K-LOVE on the radio. One day—I don't remember which, and I don't remember where—Laura Story's song "Blessings" came on. It made me wonder just where the blessing was for my dad. He was seventy-five now; was he too old to turn to Christ?

He made it through all the treatments and into his final scan. The news was clear: the cancer was still there, and surgery was the only option. He was told that he would need to have a colostomy and that the extensive surgery would require a lengthy stay in the hospital.

On the day of the surgery, my pastor was given only five minutes to see Dad while he was in pre-op. Thankfully the doctors and nurses stepped back when they began talking, and since time was short, my pastor got straight to the point. "John," he asked, "do you want to be saved?"

"Yes," said Dad.

I was prepared to wait out the entire five hours that Dad's surgery was planned to take, but after an hour I looked up to see the doctor walking toward me. I panicked, fearing the worst, but what I heard left me awed and amazed. "I can find no cancer. There is nothing there," he said. "I tattooed the area where the cancer was, and the tattoo is there, but the cancer is gone!"

A year has passed since that day, and Dad has celebrated his seventy-sixth birthday. He is cancer-free and just planted his biggest garden ever. More importantly, he is in church and loving it.

Often, when we are in the valley, we think there is no way out. But God always has a plan, and it's always for our best.

48

Family Meals

Carey Flores

I have been living here in Watertown, New York, for the past year. As an army wife, I'm used to moving from one community to another, but somehow, a couple of months ago, I just knew the Lord was calling me to become more involved with life around here. I weighed out things, trying to decide where I should put myself and with whom I should volunteer. All I ever came back with were three words: Meals On Wheels.

Eventually I got the hint and went to inquire about becoming a volunteer. They were nice and introduced me to a few of the other drivers. One of them stood out more than most: Mabel was an elderly lady in her nineties who had been serving faithfully for the past twenty-five years. I signed up right away.

The next week, with my three-year-old daughter, Zoey, in her car seat, I went back for my first day on the job. I was glad when they told me that I would be riding with the elderly lady I had met the previous week, and as we drove, we talked. She told me about some of the people we would be delivering to, but we soon started talking about her own life. I learned she was from England and had been in the Royal Air Force. She had married an American army soldier, and they settled in the United States. It was after he passed away that Mabel started volunteering with Meals On Wheels.

We'd been out for a while when I realized that I didn't know her full name. "Reome," Mabel replied.

"Really?" I said. "That's neat. How do you spell it?"

"R-E-O-M-E."

I was amazed. "That's the same last name as my dad."

Pretty soon I was in tears. As we talked, it was as if we were unraveling a secret that had been hidden for years. Mabel wasn't just a woman who happened to share my father's last name; she had been married to my grandfather's brother. She was my great aunt!

We talked more and more as we carried on delivering the meals. I heard stories of relatives I didn't know existed. There were even stories from my grandfather's funeral—a man I had never known, who had passed away almost thirty years before I was born. During our route, we had to pick up my son, Noah, from school, and Aunt Mabel could see the family resemblance in both Noah and Zoey. I went home buzzing, excited to tell my family about this amazing discovery.

I talked to my dad and one of my uncles. They were both shocked, having thought that Aunt Mabel had died years ago. To think that we all lived within three hours of one another—and me just a few miles away from Mabel—was just too much.

The next day, still smiling from it all, I told the story to my kids' teacher. She looked shocked as well; Mabel's daughter was one of her close friends. Mabel had told me she had a daughter, but I had no idea that she was a friend of "Ms. Mona."

Shortly thereafter Aunt Mabel had a doctor's appointment where it was determined that she could no longer volunteer with Meals On Wheels. But the story doesn't end there. While Aunt Mabel was absent from Meals On Wheels, she was diagnosed with cancer. She came close to losing the battle but ended up overcoming it with radiation and chemotherapy. Eventually, after not being able to volunteer with Meals On Wheels for almost a whole year, she is now back with us, having just celebrated her ninety-fifth birthday.

God's timing is perfect. Just as He was able to put the two of us in a car together at the perfect time, I know that we can trust Him with every aspect of our lives. That's why at the end of that first day when I went driving with Aunt Mabel, I wrote in my journal, "If I was not already a believer in Jesus, what happened today would have changed that. He is sooooo good! And even when I do not need proof, He continues to prove Himself to be very much alive!"

49

Snow Dog

Debra J. McDougal Ward

Seven months into our marriage Doug and I moved to Pecos, Texas. It was a new start in a new town, and we were excited to find out what God had in store for us. We didn't have much money, and since Doug drove the car to work, I spent many days alone in our low-income apartment. I tried to stay busy, but there is only so much you can do in a tiny one-bedroom apartment with hardly any furniture.

The apartment was on the edge of town, about a mile's walk to the nearest store. After it had rained one day and was cooler outside, I decided to go get a Coke. The minute I stepped outside the door of the apartment, I found in front of me the whitest dog I had ever seen. It was large, and it is only now, years later, that I realize it was a Husky.

I had not seen it around the apartments before, but it had bright eyes, and to me it looked like it was happy. It also looked like a male, so I asked him, "Hey, boy. Who do you belong to?" The dog just stared at me. I was sure that it would let me pass and go its own way once I left, so I walked away from the apartment and headed down the long road to the store. But the dog just followed me.

Because the paved road was not very wide, I thought that the dog wouldn't be safe trotting along with me, so I walked in the ditch, checking from time to time to see if my new companion was still with me. And he was. I liked this dog; I liked his happy face, the loyal way he followed me, and the fact that despite the earlier rains, he was still as white as snow. I had no idea where he had come from or how he managed not to get covered in mud, but it only made him more special.

We reached the store, and the dog waited while I went in for the Coke. I came back out to find him still sitting where I had left him, so we made our way back home, me in the ditch with the Coke and the snow dog following close behind.

Halfway back to the apartment, a car slowed down alongside me. Two men were inside. "Where you going?" one of them asked. "Do you need a ride?"

"No, I don't," I said, before adding, "thank you." I looked down and saw that the dog was now by my side, in between the car and me. The driver kept pace with me, and they both insisted I take them up on their offer.

"Is that your dog?" the driver asked.

"No," I said, feeling worried.

Immediately he stopped the car, and the passenger jumped out and hurried toward me. I was stunned and fearful and could only watch as the dog—who I had not heard make a single sound all the time he had been with me—ran in front of me, barking, and then lunged at the man. He looked startled and ran back to the car while the driver shouted, "Sure that dog is not yours!" They drove off, and I never saw them again.

I carried on, walking back to the apartment, the dog silent again, happily walking behind me. We arrived home, and I walked inside, stood in the doorway, and looked at the dog. It seemed funny and so strange that I had mud on my legs from walking along the ditch, but this dog remained as white as if he had been washed in bleach. I looked into his bright eyes and said, "I know you were sent by God to protect me from those men." The dog stood there for a moment, looked me right back in the eyes, then turned and walked off.

I walked around my apartment, praising God and thanking Him for His protection and love. After my husband got home from work, I told him what happened that day and how God protected me by sending the snow-white dog at just the right time. I wondered whether the dog belonged to someone who lived in the apartments, but after asking a few neighbors, it was clear that no one had ever seen him. I never saw the dog before that day, and I haven't seen him since.

50

Healed

John Hinkley

I'm a children's minister, and I have seen the power of prayer. I'm also a biker, so I know how bad it can hurt when your motorcycle gets wrecked. In June 2010, I saw both of those parts of my life collide in a perfect way.

I had been in a wreck that had left me with all the usual road scrapes and bruises, but there was more to it than that. X-rays revealed that I had sustained a small crack to my left hip joint, and the surgeon told me that he would have to perform surgery and place a pin in the joint to hold it together.

So I was on crutches and in pain when I next went to church to teach the children. My senior pastor wanted the kids to pray for my hip, so they all crowded around to lay their hands on me.

A few days later I was back at the hospital getting an MRI so that the surgeon would know exactly how big the crack was. Once the scan was over and I was out of the machine, the doctor walked in. "I don't know what happened," he said, "but that whole area is healed, and the crack is gone."

"I know what happened," I said. "The greatest physician in the world has healed me. His name is Jesus."

"Well," said the doctor, "I won't argue with that."

Since then, my hip has been pain-free. I have kept the old X-ray and shown it to the children, reminding them of the power of their prayers and the greatness of our God.

51

Thank You for Smiling

Mary Ann Burris

It was just a smile, but it changed my life forever. I was arriving at Wal-Mart, looking for a place to park, when a lady waved at me and flashed a big smile. I didn't recognize her, though I smiled and waved back. Then a thought came to me: maybe I should go over to her and thank her for smiling at me.

I can't do that, I thought to myself. *I don't even know her!* But the idea would not go away. I needed to go over to her and thank her for smiling at me.

I'd had these kinds of thoughts before, at random times, in different places, with various people. Each time I'd had them, they did not make sense, and they always took me out of my comfort zone, leaving me feeling vulnerable. But they had also pushed me to overcome my fears and trust God. And whenever I acted on them, something amazing always happened, the kind of thing that just wouldn't have occurred otherwise.

So I knew I had to do this. I got out of my car and walked over to the lady's vehicle. When I knocked on her door, she got out, looking at me fearfully. With my heart pounding, I blurted, "I just wanted to tell you what a beautiful smile you have and thank you for smiling at me."

She grabbed my arms and dug in. "Did God tell you that?" she asked.

"Yes," I said. "I think He did."

"You have no idea how much I needed to hear that. You see, I suffer from severe depression. The hardest thing for me is to smile. That is why I have to practice smiling. I was practicing just now when I smiled at you."

There are times when all of us wonder if God sees us and cares. That day God showed the two of us that He cares, not just about the big things but the little things too. God cared enough to act, and as a result, both of us grew to love Him more.

52

Wake Up!

Fred Hatfield

The winter wind was cold, and there was ice in our rigging. We were on board the *Little Growler*, a fishing trawler that was battling to get back to the auction at New Bedford before the bell rang for bidding to begin. But before we could unload our catch, we had some heavy seas to get through.

We had been fishing on Middle Rip and had a good haul on board, but there were northwest gale-force winds just south of Nantucket Shoals. As we entered the deep-water passage, we tied down all our gear, cleared the deck of checkers, tied open the scuppers, and put the hatch bar on. I increased the engine's RPM as much as was safe, and when the work was done, I rang the bell for the first wheel watch to take over. After the engine room had been checked, I gave instructions and put two men on wheel watch while I went forward to sleep. We were young in those days, and work was hard with very little sleep. It always seemed to me I was asleep before hitting the bunk. This time was no different as I prepared to lie down.

"Get up! There's trouble in the engine room!" The voice instantly jolted me awake, and I was out of the bunk in jig time. Looking at the clock, I saw I had only been down for ten minutes. I stopped and listened. The engine sounded good, running at the same speed as I had left it with the change of watch.

Out on the deck the lights were off. Usually when there is a call like this, the watch in the pilothouse will turn the light on, but not this time. I sat on the locker, wondering if I had dreamed the voice. But again I distinctly heard a shout from on deck: "Hurry! There's a problem in the engine room." I started to put on my socks and my boots when the voice came back, even louder and with great insistence: "Get down to the engine room now!"

I bounded up the ladder, barefoot and wearing only a T-shirt and jeans. Ice was forming on deck now, and the seas were bursting aboard as we plunged further into the north-westerly winter gale. I burst into the pilothouse. "What's wrong in the engine room?" I asked.

"What's wrong with you?" joked the man at the wheel. "Have you gone crazy, coming across the deck like that in this weather?" Opening the inspection hatch to the engine room, he peered in and said, "It looks okay to me. See for yourself."

Bypassing the watch standers, I opened the emergency hatch in the aft end of the pilothouse and slid down. Everything appeared to be normal as I stood there. The *Little Growler* was making heavy weather, bucking into the seas on the port bow, but it was normal to hear the engine strain in seas like these.

Suddenly the vessel took a lurch, and the whole electric switchboard came loose from the bulkhead. It swung once on its hinges, then broke off and fell on top of the engine. An explosion of sparks and fire cascaded over the engine and down into the bilge. A fuel injection line burst and sent out burning fuel like a flamethrower. Within two seconds, the engine room was engulfed with black smoke, the electricity was cut, and fire was everywhere. The thick black smoke covered the flames and made them hard to see, but it was impossible to ignore the heat they were giving off. The watch passed down every fire extinguisher on the vessel, and I was able to direct them to where I had perceived the flames to be when I first arrived on the scene. Eventually the fire was put out, and somehow the engine kept running. We were able to get to port.

We reviewed and discussed over and over our escape from the worst danger that can happen at sea. I asked the crew which of them had called out to me those three times. None of them had shouted out. "Besides," said one, "nothing was wrong until you arrived in the engine room."

Over and over we recounted the events, always coming to the same conclusion: without that voice waking me up and sending me to the engine room to see the accident take place, we all would have been lost. What I do know is that something—or Someone—had saved us; that was very clear.

53

Do You Believe in Divine Intervention?

Brandy Gore

"Brandy," said the doctor from behind his surgical mask, "do you believe in divine intervention?"

I did. I always had. I just wasn't expecting it that day. But God knows exactly how much we can cope with. As Psalm 139 says, He knows us before we are born. That's why God stepped in that day.

My story starts back in 2002, when—after raising my two stepchildren for six years—I became pregnant with a little girl. My joy was increased by the fact that my sister was also pregnant at the same time. Our due dates were twenty days apart, but unfortunately I found out at my first ultrasound that my little girl, Kate Ranae, was severely ill. She had Turner syndrome and a plethora of birth defects. A visit to Arkansas Children's Hospital confirmed that Kate was so ill she would not live past birth if she made it even that far. She was stillborn on December 18, 2002. Thankfully my healthy nephew, Lane, was born four days past his due date on March 9, 2003.

It took a year before I could even think about trying for another baby. I had been assured that Kate's condition was not hereditary or likely to happen again, but that didn't keep me from being nervous. Yet in February 2004, I found out I was expecting again. A first ultrasound confirmed another baby girl and reassured me that there were no signs of birth defects, and on a return visit to Arkansas Children's Hospital, I was told that I had every reason to be hopeful that this baby would be healthy.

I was due to give birth on October 5, and as spring gave way to summer, my pregnancy progressed with nothing more dramatic than moderate weight gain and the normal morning sickness and heartburn. Everything seemed fine until the early morning hours of Sunday, September 5, when my little girl woke me up. First came the hiccups, which were nothing new in this pregnancy, but next came a new sensation. She started doing what seemed like somersaults—a lot of flipping. My water broke, too, so sometime around 5:00 a.m., my husband, my parents, and I went to the hospital.

Contractions started, but because my water had broken and the labor had not progressed, I was put on medication to induce labor. I labored throughout the day and into the evening, but I was no more dilated than when I first arrived.

My doctor that day was not my regular OB-GYN, but the one on call for my clinic. But he also happened to be the same doctor who had delivered my nephew eighteen months before. He was a nice guy, very funny, and supportive, and even though I was exhausted, I felt like I was in good hands.

"I think we should perform a C-section," he said after I had been induced for twelve hours. He really was not concerned that the baby was four weeks early. His only concerns were about the risk of infection and the fact that I was pretty miserable from laboring all day. As for me, I was more than ready to have the C-section.

The surgery got underway as any normal C-section would. I lay flat while they prepped the area and could hear everything going on. I could feel the pressure of the medical team working on me, and I was shaking uncontrollably, but they reassured me that this was normal during a C-section. The anesthesiologist covered my arms with warm blankets and offered calming words of encouragement. My husband was by my head with the camera ready to snap the first picture of our daughter, but at some point during the surgery, my doctor's voice lost its happy, easygoing tone. He sounded a little tense and asked one of the nurses to bring in another doctor whose name I didn't recognize. They were moving quickly, and even though I knew something was wrong, I didn't ask them to explain. I just held on to my faith that everything was going to be okay.

That faith was confirmed when I heard the sound that every laboring mother hopes to hear: the first cries from her newborn baby's lungs. I looked up at my husband, who turned his face back to mine and, smiling, simply said, "A head full of black hair."

Then the doctor's face came into view as he leaned over the blue screen separating us and said, "Brandy, do you believe in divine intervention?" I was a little stunned by the question. What could he be talking about?

"Umm, yeah," I said.

"Your daughter had a true knot in her umbilical cord. It was a good thing that we did the C-section."

Later he explained to my family that because of the knot, the least bit of pressure could have stopped my daughter's heart from beating. If I had carried full-term, this would have been more likely. If I had tried to deliver naturally, the first push or pull would have tightened the cord. Any jerking movement while she was still inside me could have been enough to cause death.

Thankfully I did not know all these details until after I was able to finally hold my tiny baby in my arms. By the grace of God, Libby Claire was perfectly healthy in every way—five pounds, ten ounces, and nineteen inches long.

When I was pregnant with Kate, I saw God working all the time. I learned the love of friends and family, and I learned to trust. In the midst of the sorrow and pain, I found peace. With Libby, I got to witness a miracle. I was able to see God's intervention and to feel His love. I am forever thankful that I got to keep Libby. I thank Him every day for this gift.

When my father was sharing the good news about Libby's birth with friends, he put it like this: "I truly believe that God was watching over us when we lost Kate because He needed another angel in heaven, and I truly believe God was watching over us this time because He needed another angel on earth."

Whatever the reason for what we go through, God knows exactly how much we can handle.

54

The College Awakening

Derek Matthews

I was one of those freshmen who arrives at college with too much excitement and too little wisdom. I had no idea how to handle the freedom of my new life, and my eyes lit up at the thought that on any given night, I could venture off campus to one of the many open-party choices in this small college town. Somehow, in the middle of all that underage drinking and partying, I was able to maintain a decent GPA, excel in track and field, and still pass off as a nice guy who could do no harm. I felt as though I was in control of my life, and I was convinced that I was making sound decisions. I couldn't have been more wrong.

It took only one night for the tide to turn. I had gone out a little too late, drank a little too much, and wound up with the wrong crowd at the wrong time. Some people grew suspicious that drinks had been spiked, and fingers were pointed at me. Over the next few weeks I felt backed into a corner.

I searched for alibis, was pelted with threats of lawsuits, and saw a year's worth of friendships melt away. I was both angry and scared. I didn't know what to do or who to turn to.

As I was walking home from class one day, weighed down by all this stress, a fellow classmate from the same dorm approached. We made small talk for a time. When there was a pause, he asked, "Are you a Christian?"

I was a little surprised but replied, "Of course!" Growing up, I always celebrated Christmas and Easter with my family, and we attended the local church a few times a year. Of course I was a Christian; wasn't I?

"Okay," he said. "Well, do you want to join our Bible study?"

I had too few friends at college to pass up on an offer like that, so I agreed.

At the first session I felt as if everyone in the room was speaking a foreign language, but it was more than just the words everyone used; these people looked at the world differently. I tried to chime in and add to the discussion but soon recognized how little I knew about the Bible or the God I only referred to when I cussed.

That was the moment I realized something that changed my life; I had labeled myself a Christian without having a clue of what it meant or ever cracking open the Bible.

In the weeks that followed, details of that party came out, the truth emerged, and I was no longer in danger. But I didn't want to go back to the way things were. I was beginning to work out how badly I needed God in my life.

I was attending a secular, public university, and all students were required to take a humanities class that covered literature throughout the ages. The class studied Homer, Shakespeare, and John Locke, as well as sections of the Bible, which each professor explored from whatever angle he preferred. Without knowing it, I signed up for the one humanities class that was taught by a Christian.

I became fascinated by the way the professor guided his students through the Bible, looking at it from both historical and literary points of view. We explored the prophecies that announced the birth of Jesus, and with each lesson I could feel my faith growing.

God knew exactly what I needed. He provided not only a way for me to get out of the destructive scene I was in and a wise, insightful teacher who built the foundations of faith in my life, but also something I needed desperately: a friend from high school who aspired to be a pastor. We became roommates for the next two years, and it was like iron sharpening iron. We were both hungry for God, both following His compass for our lives.

All that was thirteen years ago. I'm no longer filled with anger or fear as I once was, and I realize that God showed me incredible mercy by sending good and faithful people into my life to help straighten my path. If those people had entered my life at any other point, I might have shrugged them off or resisted the lessons they were trying to reveal to me. But God knew that once I was completely broken and open to Him, I would be ready to make the best choice I have ever made: to love, trust, and follow Him.

55

Back from Death

Alan Flynt

You can tell my story in numbers, if you like. Seven: the number of minutes I was dead. Fourteen: the number of days I was in a coma. Zero: the amount of brain activity the medical staff told my family I was displaying. One: the number of miracles it took to bring me back.

I knew something was wrong in the latter half of 2013. I rarely felt well. I had trouble breathing regularly, and my fiancée, Joy, wanted me to go to the hospital to get checked out. But being the guy that I am, I just kept trying to bull my way through it.

On December 29, 2013, my father passed away at the age of ninety-four. While it can't be said I was particularly close to my father, his passing certainly affected me, and suddenly it was a whole lot harder trying to pretend that I was fine. The day after he died, I went to the funeral home to make the arrangements with my mother and sister. They, too, noticed that my breathing was becoming increasingly difficult, but everyone around me assumed it was anxiety over my dad's passing. Not me, though. By the next day I knew something was seriously wrong.

I finally drove myself to the hospital emergency room where I was admitted immediately without any waiting. The initial diagnosis was anxiety, but after several rounds of meds that changed none of my symptoms, a doctor finally came in and took a closer look.

I was kept overnight, and the next day, January 1, 2014, I was diagnosed with congestive heart failure. And they were right because later that night I had a full system shutdown. My heart stopped beating. I stopped breathing. I was gone.

After working on me for seven minutes, the staff was able to revive me. I was combative and very aggressive, so they restrained and sedated me, keeping me that way for several days. Yet when they decided to reduce the sedatives and bring me back around, nothing happened. I refused to wake up. I was in a coma.

Two weeks dragged by, and still there was no change. They carried out several EEGs to test for brain activity, but none could be found. They could see no earthly way that my situation was going to change, and my family was informed that they would have one final weekend with me to decide whether I was to be kept alive on machines or whether every-thing should be removed so that I could finally die.

I can't imagine how hard it was for them. My fiancée was a ten-hour drive away in Alabama when my heart stopped beating, and she came straight back to spend hours by my bed, staring at me, praying, hoping for a sign that something was going on inside me. One moment, without any warning, she noticed something: my eyes appeared to be moving around. It even looked to her as if I was trying to open them. Though she could not be sure, it was enough to convince her that all was not lost.

Monday morning came and with it the doctors, ready to discuss my case and talk through the idea of letting me die. That's when I opened my eyes fully for the first time.

In the following days, as the flow of doctors and nurses came and went, none could believe I was alive and awake. They called me the Miracle Man. I found it hard to hear this; I knew the reality of my life, and I was well aware of the number of mistakes and failings that had added up during my forty-five years on earth. I didn't feel very miraculous. Yet, truth be told, I knew in my heart it was true. I knew God had stepped in.

I found out that during the time I was in the coma, several churches, pastors, friends, and prayer groups were praying for me. It was humbling to hear about all the people who put their lives on hold to pray for me if only for a few minutes.

My story doesn't contain a vision or grand revelation that came to me while I was in my coma, but I do know that during the worst times, when everyone thought I was dying, I knew that I was not. I could somehow feel the hospital room vibrate with the prayers that everyone was offering up for me. It was as though my room was floating on those prayers; the presence of God was right there with me.

I spent a total of fifty days in the hospital and then rehab before I was finally sent home. Life now is pretty much as it was before, although I see my doctor regularly, take all the meds prescribed, and come home each day to my wife, Joy.

But the big change is this: I know that God is not through with me on this earth just yet. While I am still searching for what my purpose is, I take every opportunity I can to praise God for being alive and for the power of prayer.

56

Our God Is a Big God

Ashley Green

My phone vibrated on the table. I knew it would be Troy sending me a message. He had been at night class and was just ending what had been another busy day. Between working part-time, completing an internship, and starting his senior year in college, Troy did not have much time left each day. So I appreciated his messages even more.

We had been together for two months. We had met four years earlier while serving for a local ministry, and I had seen Troy grow to become a man who loved God and served with passion and humility. Whatever he did—whether working alongside urban youth to inspire and equip them or playing basketball at Arizona Christian University—he did with all his passion and all his might.

Another buzz from the table reminded me that I had not yet checked the message. I picked up the phone and read the text.

"Going to emergency because my chest is hurting really bad. I'm going to see a doctor and find out what's going on."

Troy was twenty-four, in great physical shape, and the last person you would expect to make late-night trips to the emergency room. Yes, he was busy, and the fact that he was attending school outside of his home state made him even busier than most, but that was all about to change. He was excited about finishing school in December and looking forward to having, as he said, "a little less on his plate."

He had no idea that his life was about to be turned upside down. None of us did.

When I found Troy inside the ER, he was trying hard to ignore the pain searing through his chest. He was sitting in a chair, doubled over, his head in his hands. He told me the nurses had just finished taking his vitals, and as I sat down next to him, I began to worry about what I was seeing. Troy wasn't doing much more than holding his head and breathing shallow breaths to try and minimize the pain he felt when inhaling. With every minute that passed I could see him receding more and more into himself. I felt entirely powerless. I knew the only way I could help him was to pray.

I don't know how long we waited. Time passed in strange ways, with moments when everything was busy followed by what seemed like endless pauses. I was tired. Troy was tired, but he still kept smiling, squeezing my hand to remind me that he was still here and that it was all going to be just fine. Wasn't I the one who was supposed to be doing all that?

At around 1:00 a.m., a doctor came in, followed by two nurses. They did not seem in a hurry to rush away—not like all the other times. They started out saying some things that

193

Our God Is a Big God

I don't remember now, but when they got to the point, the moment froze in time in a way that I will never forget.

"Your blood tests show that you may have a condition called lymphoma-leukemia."

"Cancer?" said Troy.

"Yes. Lymphoma-leukemia is a cancer."

The conversation carried on, with people talking about treatment and what would happen next and so many other things that I didn't hear. All I knew was that my twenty-four-year-old boyfriend had just been told that he had cancer. Cancer.

The next day was a blurry mass of doctors, X-rays, scans, and blood tests. Like a jigsaw puzzle, they gradually put together the facts until they were able to confirm that, yes, Troy's body did have cancer. Right there, in his chest, slowly wrapping itself around his heart's major arteries was a tumor the size of a grapefruit. And as far as they could tell, it was growing fast.

They told Troy that this type of lymphoma was aggressive and they wanted to start treatment right away.

"Can you operate?" Troy asked.

"No. It's too close to the heart. But we are seeing a lot of very encouraging results with chemotherapy and cancers like these."

I remember sitting at the edge of Troy's hospital bed, holding his hand and trying to think of something to say. I wanted to encourage him, to give him something to focus on, something that would help, but Troy beat me to it.

Holding up his head, his eyes looking straight at me, Troy delivered the words that I would hold on to like oxygen over the months that followed. "Our God is a big God; I know Jesus heals."

After that day my life—as well as so many others' lives—changed. The rhythms of our days were dictated by hospital schedules, treatment regimens, and a network of visitors made up of friends and family. I learned more about Troy's condition and listened carefully as the doctors explained that Troy would have a three-year journey to healing. They explained that he would need to schedule and undergo hospitalized chemotherapy treatments, radiation, and then receive further maintenance medication to ensure that the tumor wouldn't return. Overall, they told him he was looking at a three-year window before he could resume "life as usual."

Before the diagnosis the thought of having to put life on hold for three whole years would have been too much to hear. But now, with all that Troy had been through, three years sounded different.

Still, Troy kept on reminding all of us that our God is a big God and that he knew a Jesus who heals. And he didn't stop reminding us when—only three weeks after his diagnosis and one week after his first round of chemotherapy—he had to be relocated to a different state to continue his treatment with better medical technology.

Troy went through so much in those days. It wasn't just the chemo that he had to battle through; he had to complete school remotely, quit his job, and leave behind the life and friendships he had built. But his faith and optimism sparked something in all of us. Our prayers for his complete healing grew louder and louder.

It was the biggest test of Troy's life, but only twelve weeks after his original diagnosis, something happened. In a routine scan on December 12, 2012, there was no sign of the tumor at all. The doctors searched carefully, but none of them could find anything other than a normal, healthy heart and lungs. By the grace of God alone, Troy had been healed, and it didn't take three years.

It was not until January 2013, that Troy was declared in remission, and the staff still wanted him to complete his last round of chemotherapy. But they knew—as we all did—that Troy's life had been saved by a miracle. In the middle of his darkest moment, his faith burned brighter—so bright that everyone could see.

57

Esther's Rainbow

Michael Holmes

Whenever we saw a rainbow, my wife, Esther, would always want to stop and stare. If we were driving, she would have me pull over, and if there was a camera around, she would never miss an opportunity to take a photo. It wasn't just the beauty and rarity that inspired her; Esther loved the way a rainbow communicated a special message from God—how He will remember His covenant with us and all living creatures (Gen. 9:12–16 NIV).

Esther always relied on prayer and trusted God's guidance for her path in life. I can say that I am the most blessed person, not only because I knew her but also because she was my wife.

Our twelve years together started when we met in the Bronx in 2000. We were both with the police department in New York City, working in the 44th precinct, in the shadow of Yankee Stadium. Then, at 3:00 a.m. on June 3, 2012, a single phone call told me that it was all over. I listened as the caller delivered the news: "Your wife was killed in a car accident."

I am blessed to have amazing friends and family, and many of them gathered at my parents' house nearby. But in the middle of those uncontrollable emotions, I knew that only God could help me. As the dark, early-morning sky quickly turned to day, I was sitting on the back porch, admiring the view of the Hudson River, and a beautiful, bright rainbow appeared. It was as if God was telling me that Esther was with Him and doing just fine.

As the days passed, the rainbows kept appearing, and different people told me about the ones they had seen. I hadn't told anyone about their significance to Esther, and now to me, but people kept bringing up rainbows in conversations. Esther's old partner from work showed up to our house with pictures of a rainbow on the same day that my sister and her family showed up from Ohio, wanting to show me the picture of a rainbow they saw in south New Jersey during their eight-hour drive. I even read a blog about a double rainbow that appeared in Manhattan on the day Esther passed away.

Tuesday came and with it the start of the wake. Hundreds of family, friends, and police coworkers showed up. Some of them I knew well, others I had not seen before, and some told me they had waited over an hour in line. One unknown man stepped up and introduced himself as someone who had met Esther only once but felt compelled to wait in line and pay his respects. I hugged him and thanked him for coming. "By the way," he said, just before he turned to go, "I was getting off the parkway, and I saw an amazing rainbow."

I almost fell down. "Why did you just say that?" I asked. He looked nervous, worrying that he had upset me. But I assured him that in fact his words had given me nothing but comfort.

The next day carried on with more of the same: more friends, more family, and more rainbows. On the day of Esther's funeral, Yankee Stadium sat beneath a blazing arc of color—a perfect rainbow standing in the very precinct where Esther and I had first met.

For weeks to come I saw or heard about amazing and beautiful rainbows. Even the weather and news reports in New York picked up on the fact that there were many more rainbows than usual that summer. And every time I looked to the sky to see those beautiful arcs of color, I knew God was reminding me that He loves me, that He is always with me. And until I see my Esther again, I'll never forget that.

58

Restored and Redeemed

Samir Aziz

I used to see my father once a year. I looked forward to those visits more than I ever looked forward to Christmas or the end of another horrendous year of school. For me, a young boy living with his mother and older sister in a large town in the south of England, the days when we would drive to the airport and watch the exotically dressed passengers sweep out of arrivals provided me with some of my most vivid and precious childhood memories. I would wait for my dad, knowing to ignore the men wearing their long white robes and headscarves. Though my dad lived in the Middle East, he dressed as sharp as a city banker.

My dad was a Muslim, and my mom wasn't quite a Christian. He had decided to stay in Abu Dhabi while she wanted to live in England. Maybe that's why I didn't ever know where I belonged. I was bullied at school, and my teenage years were a one-way journey toward self-destruction. I tried drinking, drugs, and petty crime and pushed so many boundaries that I lost all sense of perspective. I was kicked out of my house. Then I was kicked out of the next house. I tried to commit suicide. I was kicked out of another house.

I ended up moving out to live with my dad in Abu Dhabi when I was fifteen. A dream come true? In some ways, but my cycle of self-destruction continued over there. My dad was unemployed, had no money, and was in debt to many people. I fell in with a bad crowd, got involved with some bad things, and got myself kicked out of yet another home.

By the time I went to live with my uncle in Bahrain, I was ready for a change. He spoke very little English, and I spoke very little Arabic, but we got along well enough. And when he invited me to join him at his mosque, I felt I had nothing to lose. I grew to love Islam, and I became deeply committed to my faith.

When I turned seventeen, I returned to England. I was no longer the rebel without a cause. I was focused, devout, religious. Even though I was the only Muslim in my neighborhood, I prayed five times a day, observed all the religious festivals, and saw myself as a peace-loving evangelist for Mohammed.

I landed a great job and fell in love with Debi, a beautiful English woman. We got engaged, though the wedding took a while to follow. Within a few years of being married, we had two wonderful sons. I thought that life was set for me, that I would continue to thrive at work, and that eventually Debi would see the truth in all I had been telling her about my faith and convert to Islam too.

I was at work when Debi called me. She had been feeling unwell for some time and had gone to the hospital for tests, but even so I was surprised to hear her crying on the phone.

"What is it?" I asked. "What did they say?"

"Cancer," she replied. "I have bladder cancer."

I felt strong, not worried. "Allah will heal you," I said. "I'll pray."

Debi was young to get this kind of cancer, and the doctors wanted to operate straightaway. As we so often do in times of fear, Debi turned to faith for comfort. But not my faith. Her mom was a strong Christian, and on the night before Debi was due to go in to surgery, she invited her along to church. I stayed home, but the minute Debi walked back through the door, I could tell something had happened. "They prayed for me in the name of Jesus," she said. "And there was this heat that rushed from head to toe."

Jesus? Just hearing her mention His name made me mad. I sat and listened as she talked some more, feeling only anger boiling like hot lava within me.

The next day the surgery started as planned, but when the surgeons got to the bladder, they could find none of the cancer that the pre-op scans had revealed. It was amazing news, and for both Debi and me it was clear that our prayers had been answered. Only, I was convinced that Allah had done the healing while she and her family gave all the glory to Jesus.

Debi started taking the boys to church every week. I sat at home, feeling wounded, angry, and lost. It was hard to hear them talk about Jesus, hard to see the way they would return home so happy on Sunday mornings. I started to feel isolated and alone, not knowing where I belonged, just as I had felt when I was a teenager. I felt as though I was a battleground, torn between loving my family and feeling pushed away by their newfound faith. About the only thing that kept me in the relationship was the fact that I was desperate that my boys would not live in a repeat of my own childhood.

So I stuck it out. I watched as Debi's and the boys' faith grew. I listened as they talked about what happened at church. I even went along to Debi's baptism—sitting in the front row, a human mass of tension and anger. All I wanted was to disappear.

Something had to give. Two years after Debi's healing, I was alone at home one day. The rage within me had gotten to be too much, and no matter how much I paced up and down, I couldn't find any relief. Eventually I fell to my knees on the bathroom floor. "Jesus," I called out, "if You really are real and You really do exist, then come into my life."

I remember thinking that it was odd—wrong, even—for a Muslim like me to be praying to Jesus, but I did it anyway. I kept calling out Jesus' name, asking Him to come and show up, to change something, to rescue me. I kept on and on at Him until at some point I noticed that the light in the room had changed. It was as if someone had put floodlights in the bathroom, and this bright light just kept on growing. Then the tears came. I cried and cried as I had never cried before, and while I know now that my sins were being washed away, at the time all I knew was that I couldn't stop the tears.

I didn't tell anyone about what happened that day. I just carried on, almost as usual. But inside I was suddenly fascinated by Jesus. I borrowed Debi's Bible and read through the book of Revelation. I was hungry, and only God could satisfy. When I was involved in a car accident one winter morning, something changed. It was cold, and my little hatchback was no match for either the ice or the SUV that I collided with. Even though I broke my fibula, fractured my tibia, damaged ligaments, broke ribs, and narrowly missed losing my sight in one eye when a whole load of glass embedded itself in my forehead, the emergency services said I was lucky to survive the crash. But none of these was the most significant thing about the accident. What impacted me the most were the words that clearly went through my mind as I sailed toward the Land Rover: "Jesus! I can't die—I've only just found You."

I couldn't deny it to myself any longer. I was a Christian. I told Debi, and I started going to church. I got baptized and soaked myself in sermons and worship music whenever I was driving alone in the car. I was in love with Jesus. I was giving Him my life.

Today I am passionate about my faith. I am bold and want to make disciples of all nations. I want to see souls saved from every culture. I speak to Muslims about what happened to me, and I tell them how, after half a lifetime of searching in all the wrong places—from drugs to alcohol, crime to suicide, Islam to self-hatred—there's only one place, one Person who truly has the answer. His name is Jesus.

Afterword

We chose "Restored and Redeemed" as the last story in *It's a God Thing, Volume 2* because we truly believe the most amazing miracle of all is that God saves people, just like Samir Aziz, every day and that the three greatest words in all the world are *I love you*—which God so eloquently says to us through the gift of His Son.

For God so loved the world that He gave His only begotten Son, that whoever believes in Him should not perish but have everlasting life. (John 3:16 NKJV)

For readers who don't have a relationship with God through Jesus, we pray that these stories have persuaded you of His love and His power in the lives of His children and that you will come to know and love Him as we do.

And for those who are experiencing difficult circumstances, in the book of Job there is a verse that speaks of courage that comes from hope (Job 11:18 NLT). It is our prayer that these stories infuse you with the hope that comes from a relationship with Jesus and the courage to live your life for His glory.

About the Writer

Craig Borlase is a writer living in the UK. He has coauthored twenty-one books and has written five books, including *The Naked Christian*, *William Seymour: A Biography*, and *2159 AD: A History of Christianity*.

Born in 1972, Craig grew up attending church, editing a Christian magazine, and eventually becoming a little cynical about things he didn't really understand.

"It was about the time when the organization I was involved with grew really big that I felt the need to write something that exposed what I saw as the problems with the church. It turned out that I was wrong: *The Naked Christian* was all about my own problems—my narrow view of faith, my weakness, my inconsistency, my arrogance."

After a two-year break to teach high school English, Craig spent his early thirties working on his own books as well as writing for an international development agency. The experiences dramatically shaped his faith, as did the rites of birth and bereavement as his family grew on one end and shrunk on the other.

"I feel as though I spent my teens trying to get a buzz out of faith (or drugs), my twenties waiting around for someone to give me permission to take that faith seriously, and my thirties stripping away the nonsense and discovering the power of God's grace and love for myself. Now that I've turned forty, I'm realizing that one of the reasons I'm here is simply to find the good things that God is doing and help share the news with others. The older I get, the better life becomes."

Today Craig writes collaboratively with a range of publishers and authors. His most recent project is *Row for Freedom*, Julia Immonen's story of her record-breaking row across the Atlantic Ocean to raise awareness of the extent of human trafficking.

About the Creators

Don Jacobson has enjoyed working in the publishing industry for more than thirty years. He leads the team at D. C. Jacobson & Associates (DCJA), an author management company, working with authors and dreaming about books that change the world. Don's first collection of stories, *When God Makes Lemonade: True Stories That Amaze & Encourage*, was published by Thomas Nelson in 2013, and the first volume of *It's a God Thing* was published in January 2014.

A graduate of Multnomah University in Portland, Don lives with Brenda, his wife of thirty-six years, in Fairview, Oregon.

K-LOVE creates compelling media that inspires and encourages listeners to have a more meaningful relationship with Christ. Our hope is that what you experience through K-LOVE will deepen your relationship with Christ and help you understand His love for you and the amazing purpose that He has for your life.

> "For I know the plans I have for you," declares the LORD, "plans to prosper you and not to harm you, plans to give you hope and a future." (Jer. 29:11 NIV)

The radio network has 500 signals in 47 states, with an estimated weekly audience of 14 million. For more information visit www.klove.com.

WE WANT TO HEAR YOUR STORY . . .

Did reading these miracle stories help you remember a time that God acted—perhaps in your life? Maybe it's time to share that story—it just may be the thing someone needs to give him or her the courage to hang on and believe in God for a miracle.

SO WHAT IS YOUR GOD THING STORY?

It's always encouraging to hear stories of God at work in our lives, and we can't wait to hear yours! If you have never written anything, don't let that stop you—we have a writer who will help you tell your story.

If you would like to submit a story to be considered for our next volume of *It's a God Thing*, please visit our website at http://itsagodthing.com.

You can also follow us on Twitter (@IAGTMiracles) or like us on Facebook (http://facebook.com/itsagodthingmiracles).

It's a God Thing stories are modern-day miracle stories—stories that simply can't be explained in any other way other than it was God's divine intervention.

Did you enjoy the stories you just read in *It's a God Thing, Volume 2*?

Then you will also be interested in reading *It's a God Thing, Volume 1: When Miracles Happen to Everyday People*, which contains forty-eight miracle stories, including angel appearances in hospital rooms to a mother saved from a would-be assailant in Hyde Park, from a young autistic girl becoming a beautiful ballerina overnight to a young back-packer who walked away from a terrorist attack, *It's a God Thing, Volume 1* presents some of the most amazing stories of God's hand on our lives.

Be motivated as never before to look for and witness the incredible ways that God is interacting in your life and the lives of those around you.

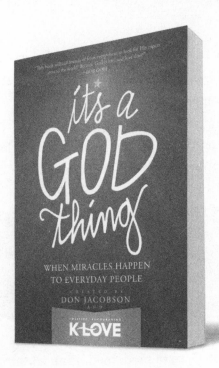

 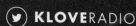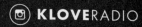

K-LOVE: It IS a God Thing

God things are unexplainable. God things are also miraculous, wonderful, life affirming, and soul sustaining.

Clearly, what began humbly in 1982, as a single radio station in Santa Rosa, California, and has grown to a media empire of more than 500 stations from coast to coast that inspires more than 15 million listeners each week *is* a God thing. By providing positive music and inspirational stories, K-LOVE helps people draw closer to God, know God, and walk through every day of their lives *with* God.

Music is our tool, but the message of K-LOVE is far greater. Our mission is to effectively communicate the gospel to those who do not know or fully understand it while also helping those walking with Jesus Christ to grow stronger in their relationships with Him.

From music and inspirational stories to interviews with Christian artists and partnerships with Christian charities, K-LOVE is dedicated to serving Jesus Christ 24 hours a day, 7 days a week, 365 days a year, on-air and online. Behind the scenes K-LOVE's full-time ministry team processes more than one hundred phone calls a day from listeners seeking support and guidance. The pastors and staff at K-LOVE pray for more than a thousand prayer requests every day.

We are a ministry of believers with hearts for Jesus Christ and a love for serving others. We, like you, hear God through His Word and other believers whose personal testimonies showcase the powerful works He is doing in our lives. We hope this collection of stories will inspire you to look for God in your daily life, from your major triumphs, where His voice is loud and clear, to the small blessings, where His Holy Spirit quietly guides you to fulfill His purpose for your life.

K-LOVE creates compelling media designed to inspire and encourage people to develop meaningful relationships with Christ.

K-LOVE is listener supported and delivers positive, encouraging, contemporary Christian music through its five hundred signals across forty-seven states. For more information visit: www.klove.com.

POSITIVE, ENCOURAGING

K-LOVE.

Connect with K-LOVE . . .

Website:	klove.com
Facebook:	Facebook.com/kloveradio
Twitter:	@kloveradio
Instagram:	@kloveradio
Google +:	+K-LOVE
Pinterest:	pinterest.com/kloveradio
YouTube:	youtube.com/kloveradio
Phone:	1.800.525.LOVE (5683)
Email:	klove@klove.com

God is changing lives through Christian Radio – thanks for sharing the vision!

Our Values . . .

We Trust in God - Our faith, trust, and hope is in Christ. God's Word guides our decisions, refreshes us, and creates an unshakable faith. Our dependence on God is reflected in our commitment to prayer.

Create an Extraordinary Impact - We serve an extraordinary God who deserves our all. He allows us to create, produce, and share media with His life-changing message.

We are Passionate, Creative, and Have Fun - Innovative ideas and solutions, individual initiative, and having a good time make our work and lives more interesting.

Learn, Improve, and Grow - We challenge and stretch ourselves, each other, and the ministry to realize the full potential God has given us.

In His Strength - It's not about us.

Do you know someone who could use some encouragement? Perhaps that someone is you.

When *God Makes Lemonade* comes from the lives of everyday folk—a collection of stories about people like you who have discovered unexpected sweetness in the midst of sour circumstances.

Some of these real-life stories are laugh-out-loud funny, others are sobering, and more than a few will have you reaching for a tissue. But these true stories all have one thing in common: hope.

There is no question; life will sometimes give you *lemons*; out-of-your-control issues of health, employment, and relationships, circumstances that are truly sour—you wouldn't wish them on anyone.

But when those lemons become lemonade . . . it is as refreshing as an ice-cold drink on a hot summer day.

When in life "stuff happens," know that Lemonade Happens™ too! Be encouraged and inspired . . . *When God Makes Lemonade.*

If you have a Lemonade story to tell, please visit us at:

Website: www.godmakeslemonade.com
Facebook: www.facebook.com/godmakeslemonade
Twitter: @LemonadeHappens